REMEMBERING MICHAEL
A Mother's Story

Mrs Jackson's Memoir

Edition 2
Copyright© 2024 All rights reserved. Solo Inc.

All rights reserved, including the right to reproduce this book or portions thereof in any form.
Second Edition.
Story Narration on Behalf of: Katherine Jackson
ISBN: 9798302475862

Disclaimer: No part of this eBook may be reproduced, stored, or transmitted in any form or by any means, including mechanical or electronic, without prior written permission from the author. While the author has made every effort to ensure that the ideas, statistics, and information presented in this Book are accurate to the best of their knowledge, any implications—whether direct, derived, or perceived—should be understood and applied at the reader's discretion. The author cannot be held liable for any personal or commercial damage resulting from the communication, application, or misinterpretation of the information contained herein. All rights reserved.

Preface

This book is a tribute to Mrs. Katherine Jackson, the matriarch of the Jackson family. It features rare photographs from the family's private album and personal stories shared by Mrs. Jackson about Michael and their family.

Throughout Mrs. Jackson's life, many details about Michael were kept private. Now, several years after his passing, she shares these stories in the hope of revealing who Michael truly was.

This updated edition includes new insights from Mrs. Katherine Jackson, as well as contributions from other family members and close friends. It offers a deeper understanding of Michael, moving beyond the media's portrayal of him as a meteoric pop star.

In her own words, Mrs. Jackson describes Michael as "compassionate, kind, generous, and humble"—a son whose remarkable acts of kindness were central to his true legacy.

The purpose of this book is to echo Mrs. Jackson's sentiment: to honor and celebrate the extraordinary humanitarian Michael was, and to recognize the incredible impact his art had on the world during his fifty short years—and beyond.

This new edition has been thoughtfully expanded from its original memoir, drawing from heartfelt interviews that weave together a rich and vivid tapestry of Michael's memory.

Michael's music brought inspiration and joy to millions, uniting people across cultures with his messages of love, hope, healing, social justice, equality, fun, innocence, and celebration. His impact will endure for generations.

The process of working with Katherine Jackson on this project has been a profound experience. In countless hours of conversation, she revealed intimate stories as the matriarch of one of music's most famous families—many members of whom are legends in their own right.

Mrs. Jackson's resilience and grace, despite the immense challenges she faced—the loss of her husband, Joseph, and three children (Brandon, Michael, and Tito)—are truly inspiring. Katherine Jackson's maternal strength is the foundation of the Jackson family.

This book is dedicated to the late Joseph Jackson and Tito Jackson, both of whom shared cherished anecdotes about Michael that appear throughout its pages.

In addition to the intimate stories, this book features hundreds of photographs from the Jackson family archive, including rare illustrations hand-drawn by Michael himself.

Finally, thank you, Michael, for your inspiration. May your remarkable legacy live on forever.

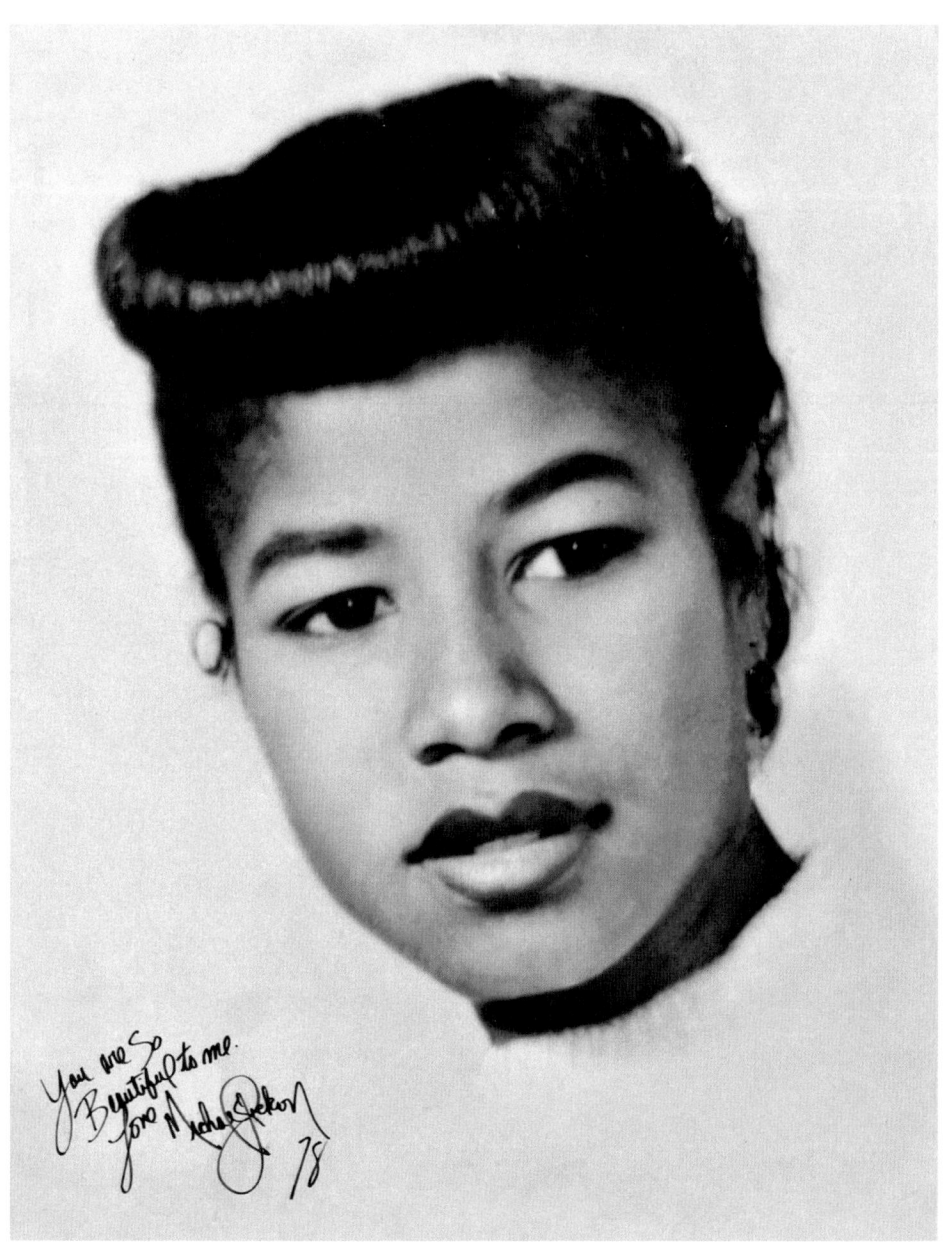

I've always known that my son Michael had talent, but I never imagined he would reach the heights of success he achieved. My husband, Joseph, and I both grew up with a deep love for music, so it's no surprise that it was passed on to our children.

As a child, I grew up in small towns in Barbour, Alabama, and later Ferriday, Louisiana. Music was a staple in my life. I played the clarinet in school and enjoyed singing with my little sister, Hattie. But everything changed when I met a young man, Joseph Jackson.

Joseph played guitar in a band with his brother called The Falcons. After we got married and had nine children; Rebbie, Jackie, LaToya, Tito, Jermaine, Marlon, Michael, Randy and Janet. We moved to a small house at 2300 Jackson Street in Gary, Indiana. Our home was buzzing with the sounds of country, blues, and jazz—music that all of our children loved, especially, Michael.

From a young age, Michael had natural rhythm. As a baby, he loved music and dancing. I remember him sitting on our rickety, old washing machine with a bottle in his mouth, grooving to the noise of the rinse cycle. It was amusing to watch him as a child.

Our family loved music, we would sing country songs together. I remember when our TV broke and we couldn't afford to fix it, we gathered the family together to sing songs. We sang tunes from our favorite artists, like The Temptations and James Brown. With Joseph's hobbies we always had guitars and other instruments around the house. Our son Tito was one of the first of our boys to take interest. He borrowed Joseph's guitar to practice while Joseph worked long hours at the steel mill. One day, Tito broke a guitar string. When Joseph came home from work, he was upset. He told Tito to play in our living room to show him what he had learned. It was that day when Joseph had the vision. He recognized our sons' many talents and formed the first family band, The Jackson Brothers, with Tito, Jackie, and Jermaine as the lead vocalist.

At first, Michael and Marlon weren't part of the group because Joseph thought they were too young. That changed when I heard Michael singing one day while making his bed. I begged my husband to listen to Michael sing, but Joseph refused. It wasn't until we both heard Michael sing "Climb Every Mountain" in his school choir that Joseph changed tune. It was around 1964 when Joseph allowed Marlon and Michael to join their older brothers, in the group and renamed it The Jackson Five.

> **Before Michael could speak, he could sing harmony and he could dance. Nobody ever taught him to do that. I don't know where it came from, he was just able to do it.**

After many months of training and practice, Joseph knew our boys had real potential. He bravely cut back on his shifts at the steel mill to devote more time to the band. It was a bold move, but he had faith. My husband wanted our children to achieve greatness and accomplish things he hadn't been able to as a musician. Growing up in Gary at that time was financially difficult; there weren't many opportunities for youth.

Our family had humble beginnings. I don't know where we'd be if it weren't for Joseph's ambition and his vision for our future.

7

Left to Right: Michael, Randy, Joseph

Left: Jermaine, Marlon, Jackie, Tito and Michael

Left to Right: Jackie, Michael, and Randy surrounded by family and friends

Left to Right: Michael, Marlon, Jermaine and Tito

Left to Right: Michael, Marlon, Jackie and Randy

Left: 2300 Jackson Street, Gary, Indiana

Joseph and me, backstage

With Joseph as their manager, the boys began performing at local talent shows around Gary and Chicago, quickly gaining attention and opening for musical acts that were often twice their age.

In 1967, Joseph took the boys to perform at amateur night at the Apollo Theatre in New York, where they sang Smokey Robinson's "Who's Lovin' You." Mrs. Gladys Knight, who was performing with The Pips, heard Michael's voice from her dressing room and immediately wanted to meet the boys. At the time, Mrs. Knight was signed to Motown Records, working with Mr. Berry Gordy, and she wanted to help the boys get a record deal.

My boys had dreamed of joining Motown since we were back in Gary, but they had heard that Mr. Gordy wasn't interested in signing another young act, especially after Stevie Wonder had already signed with the label. However, thanks to Mrs. Gladys Knight and Mr. Bobby Taylor of The Vancouvers, Mr. Gordy agreed to let the boys audition for him, poolside at his home. After their performance, they were signed on the spot. Mr. Taylor then brought them into the studio to record their first album under Motown Records. It was a dream come true for the whole family.

In 1968, Joseph decided to move the family to California. He bought an old tour bus so they could travel and perform across the country for long stretches of time. Of course, I stayed behind in Gary with our other children—Janet, LaToya, Rebbie, and Randy. It wasn't until 1971 that we finally bought a bigger home in Encino, and the whole family was reunited.

The Encino estate was beautiful, but it felt empty when the boys and Joseph were on tour, which was often. I missed our family dinners, and sometimes I wished we were back in Gary, when life was simple and we were all together.

I remember telling the boys before they became famous to never let fame go to their heads. Having a good image was important. Mr. Gordy and Joseph worked together to help build their Motown image. Sadly, after a few years, the boys outgrew Motown and wanted more control over their sound. They felt it was time for a change.

Leaving Motown in 1975 was a tough decision. The boys were scouted by Ronald Alexenberg and Walter Yetnikoff at Epic Records (CBS) and signed a new contract, under a new name, The Jacksons.

Michael was eager to write his own songs and collaborated with talented songwriters like Gamble and Huff. Their new record deal also included a TV variety special featuring the whole family. Soon, we found ourselves overwhelmed with weekly rehearsals, preparing skits and performances with big stars like Sonny and Cher, Red Foxx, and Joey Bishop, just to name a few.

The show was a success, but after one exhausting season, the boys decided to quit the show and return to making music. They preferred traveling the world and performing for their fans, rather than spending hours a day filming a television show in a studio. The boys went back to what they loved most—performing music.

> **I missed our family dinners and sometimes wished we were back in Gary, when life was simple.**

Left: Tito, Jackie, Marlon, Leon Huff, Kenneth Gamble, Michael and Randy

Left: Tito, Marlon, Jackie, and Micahael performing in stage costumes designed by Ruthie West

Left: Rebbie, Jackie, Janet, LaToya, Micahael and Randy on set of The Jacksons Variety Show

Left: Jackie, Tito, Michael, Marlon and Jermaine

Even though most people saw my son as a star, at home, Michael was just a regular kid. When he was younger, we gave him an allowance, which he spent on candy. He would set up a little store in front of our house to give the candy away. There was always a generous spirit about Michael. What he cared about most was other people.

When Michael was on stage, he did things you wouldn't expect a child his age to do. Michael surprised us with his ability to sing with such deep emotion. When Joseph and I heard him sing for the first time in his school choir, we were both shocked. We couldn't understand how Michael could sing those lyrics with such feeling, considering he hadn't lived through any of those experiences yet.

From a young age, Michael knew how he wanted his music to sound and feel. Growing up, he spent several hours in the studio, recording both background and lead vocals. He often stayed at the studio longer than his brothers. It was a sacrifice, but he really had a passion for recording.

Even at a young age, Michael wanted everything to be perfect. He wouldn't release any music unless it was the best it could be. That's just how Michael was, and that's what he achieved with his music. He was different on stage than he was off. Offstage, he was shy and not very talkative, but when he stepped on stage, everything opened up for him. The stage was where he felt at home.

When Michael was touring with his brothers, I saw him less and less, but his father was with him most of the time. I felt there was too much pressure placed on Michael when he was young, and it saddens me to know that he resented some aspects of his childhood. I've heard him say he never had a childhood. I don't agree with that, but I accept that it's how he felt.

Michael worked a lot, but he also had time off with his brothers to enjoy childhood. Yes, he made sacrifices, but most of the neighborhood kids in Gary weren't at the playground anyway—they were at our house watching the boys rehearse through the window. I didn't know Michael was suffering as much as he said he was.

> **If I could do it all again, I would make sure that Michael had more time to enjoy his childhood, and didn't work all the time.**

As parents, Joseph and I felt we were did right by our children. If I could do it all again, I would make sure that Michael had more time to enjoy his childhood and didn't have to work so much. It's hard to live with regret, because I know he did exactly what he loved.

Our family grew up with music. My children loved performing and supported one another, as a family should. When Michael went solo at Motown, we all knew this was what he wanted to do. Michael knew he wouldn't have achieved everything he did without hard work and dedication as a child. I've heard Michael express his frustration about the sacrifices he made, but I know he had some childhood—just not a regular one. That's just how it is when you're in show business.

When my boys became famous, it was important to me that they remained humble and didn't let fame go to their heads. I often told my boys to never boast about what they did and to never forget where we came from.

Left: Michael, Tito, Marlon, Jermaine and Jackie on the basketball court

Left: Tito, Marlon, Jackie, Michael, and Jermaine rehearsing on stage

Left: Jackie and Michael   Right: Michael in flight

Left: Tito, Marlon, Michael, Jackie and Jermaine at a photo shoot

Michael, Jackie, Randy and Tito, meeting the Royal Family

The day my children surprised me with a brand new, Rolls Royce

Aside from the music, what made me most proud of Michael was his generous heart and giving nature. In the early days, Michael learned about the world by watching television, or sometimes I would take him to a local museum to learn about history. But once the boys became famous and started touring, traveling became Michael's real education.

Due to their hectic showbiz schedules, the boys could no longer attend regular school, so we hired a tutor, Mrs. Fines, to teach them while they were on the road.

Michael was very fond of his instructor. He was a good student who loved learning as much as he loved music. Mrs. Fines would take Michael to museums in different countries, enriching his understanding of the world. I remember that Michael even bought a piano as a gift for her—he simply adored her.

I'll never forget the day Michael and I were watching TV when a public service announcement about the poor, starving children in Africa aired. Seeing those children in the commercial brought us both to tears. I remember Michael, who was young at the time, making a promise to me: "One day, Mother, I'm going to do something about this."

When he grew older, Michael kept that promise. While on a trip to New York City, he surprised me by taking me to an airport hangar, where he had arranged for hundreds of boxes of food, goods, and emergency supplies to be loaded onto several planes, ready to take off for Africa. I was so proud to see my son follow through on his words.

Michael's generosity didn't stop there. He dedicated many years to supporting charities and working with disabled children. His commitment to giving back earned him a spot in the Guinness Book Of World Record for supporting the most charities as a celebrity.

As a devout Jehovah's Witness, Michael and I often did service work together, going door-to-door. However, after he gained fame, it became difficult for Michael to perform this service; even in a full disguise, with wigs and glasses, people would still recognize him.

So instead, Michael found different ways to serve his community. Sometimes, he would go out at night with his driver, giving away hundred-dollar bills to strangers he met while in town.

Michael was also incredibly generous with his family. Although we didn't celebrate birthdays my children would sometimes organize small celebrations at our home. One year, they even hired my favorite country musician, Floyd Cramer, to perform. I remember a few days before the party, my daughter Janet asked me what my favorite color was, and I could tell she was up to something fishy.

During the party, Michael handed me a big red ribbon and told me to follow it to the end. The ribbon led me all the way outside to the parking lot, where I found a brand-new, shiny red Rolls-Royce with a big bow on top.

I couldn't believe my children had bought me that car. It was a moment that made me realize just how far we had come.

> **"When Michael was young, he promised 'One day, Mother, I'm going to do something to help the starving children in Africa.' Years later, he kept that promise.**

Right: Michael, Marlon, Jackie and Tito with the USAF Thunderbirds

Right: Randy and Michael on tour in Japan

Right: Red Foxx, Randy and Michael on the set of The Jackson's Variety Show

Right: Tito, Marlon, Jermaine, Michael and Jackie

Michael adored Hollywood icons such as Elizabeth Taylor and Diana Ross. They were both inspirations to him and, also, friends.

I was surprised when Michael married Lisa Marie Presley, but I was happy to know that she made him happy, and that's all a mother could ever want. If Michael was happy, I was happy too. I remember when called me after it was in the news that they got married, and I asked him to put Lisa on the phone so I could hear her voice. I almost didn't believe it was her, but we developed a great friendship soon after, and she would come by the house to visit me often. It was a Southern tradition, and being from the South, I really appreciated that Lisa Marie shared my values.

Michael was a big Elvis fan. He adored all the great artists of our time—like Fred Astaire, Gregory Peck, and Yul Brynner, who were also among his closest friends. In fact, Michael often brought random celebrities to visit, unannounced. I'll never forget the time he barged in with Yul Brynner late at night, and I was wearing my nightcap. I remember being so embarrassed.

Michael didn't have a normal childhood growing up, but he had his brothers. Marlon and Michael were closest because of their age, and he admired his big brother, Jermaine. Tito was everyone's favorite because of his fun-loving spirit, and he was very supportive.

Michael was also close to his sisters, but mostly Janet and LaToya, since Rebbie was much older.

Michael and LaToya grew even closer as siblings when they shared an apartment in New York while he was performing on The Wiz in 1978, with Quincy Jones and Diana Ross. LaToya sang backup for Michael for years and appeared in his videos like "Say, Say, Say" and "The Way You Make Me Feel." Michael was the big brother to Janet and a big fan of her music. Janet looked to Michael as a mentor, and they respected one another musically.

Our family moved to Encino in 1971, but in the 1980s, we wanted to sell and relocate to Hollywood. However, after months of searching, we couldn't find a suitable home. Instead, my husband and Michael decided to remodel our Encino home. Rather than making a few small changes, Michael tore the entire house down and rebuilt it into my dream home, knowing that I really adored the English-style Tudor estates of those days.

> **" I was surprised when Michael married Lisa Marie Presley, but I was happy for them, because I know she made him happy.**

In the yard outside, Michael added a beautiful guest house with a candy shop, a gazebo, a koi pond, and a pool. He built a studio above the garage where he could practice his dancing without anyone bothering him. Michael created "Billie Jean," "Beat It," and "Don't Stop 'Til You Get Enough" at the house.

It wasn't until the 1990s, when Michael was 30, that he decided to move to Neverland Ranch. I knew it was coming, but I wasn't happy. I never told him this, but when he left, I cried. I'm the type of mother who never wants her children to leave the home.

Left-to-Right: Jackie, Jermaine, Tito, Marlon and Michael

Left-to-Right: Randy, Michael, Tito and Marlon at a high-school ceremony

Joseph and The Jackson Five on tour in Australia. posing with their fans.

Whenever my boys returned home from traveling the world, they always had so many stories to share about their experiences abroad, which was always exciting.

I know that Joseph tried to instill cultural values in our family, teaching the boys to respect all races and religions. Traveling the world was a great source of education and inspiration for Michael and his brothers. I remember one story my sons shared from their Jackson Five Australian tour back in 1974.

While promoting their album in Australia, the boys visited a local school in a small town to perform for the children. During the performance, Joseph noticed a group of Native American fans standing outside, which piqued his curiosity. He soon learned that racial segregation existed in the area, and these children were not allowed to meet the boys or take any photos.

This upset Joseph, and he insisted that no fans be discriminated against. He asked the school principal to allow the fans in to meet the boys, or the event would be canceled. The principal agreed, and the young fans were allowed to watch the performance. I believe this incident had a lasting impact on Michael, because years later, he returned to Australia on a mission to help children from Indigenous communities.

Not many people know this, but whenever Michael toured, he would arrange his schedule to visit parts of the world where he felt his concerts could provide work and income for local crews, even if only for a short time.

In every city, Michael also made it a priority to stop by local hospitals to visit sick children and find ways to help. He personally paid for numerous medical surgeries for terminally ill children when their parents couldn't afford the bills. He also covered funeral costs for children who had passed away, to ensure their families could give them an honorable burial.

I believe one of the reasons Michael wrote songs like "Heal the World" and "I'll Be There" is because he believed the lyrics of a song could be healing and powerful. Michael wanted to create music that evoked the joy, love, innocence, and magic he saw in children— that's why they were his biggest inspiration.

> **Michael wanted to create music that evoked the joy, love, innocence and magic he saw in children; that's why they were his greatest inspiration.**

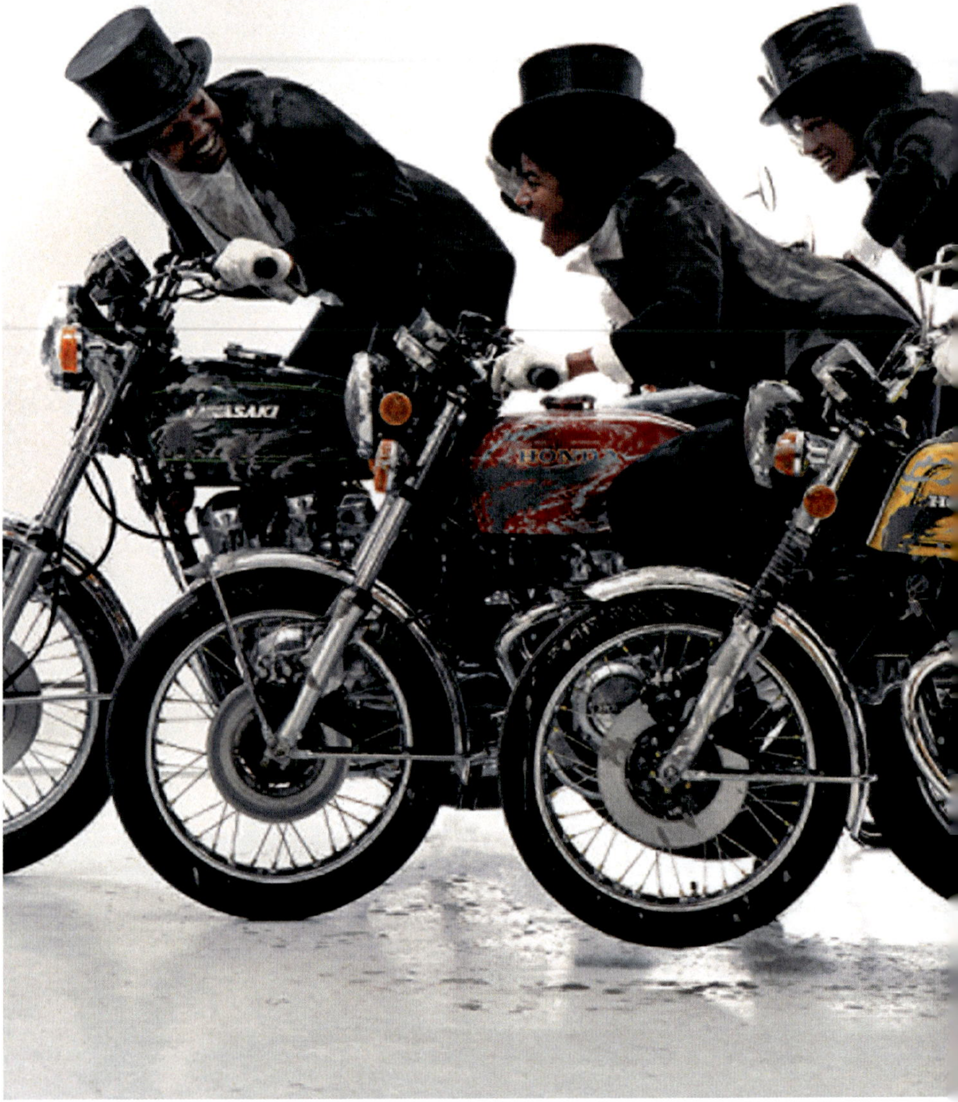

The Jacksons CBS/Epic Years.

Left: Michael, Randy, Jackie, Marlon and Tito; Right: Jermaine and Michael.

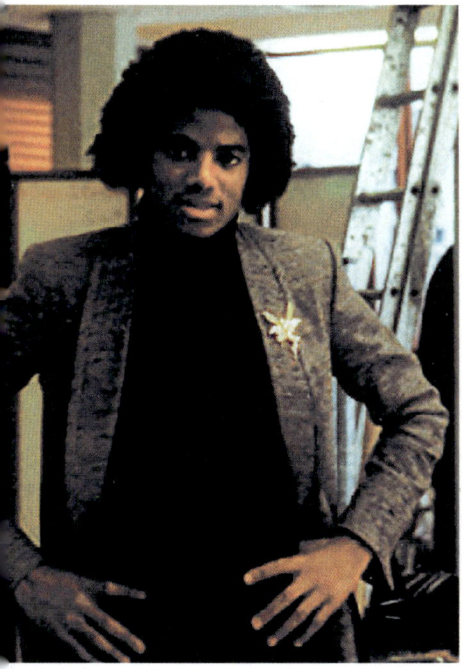

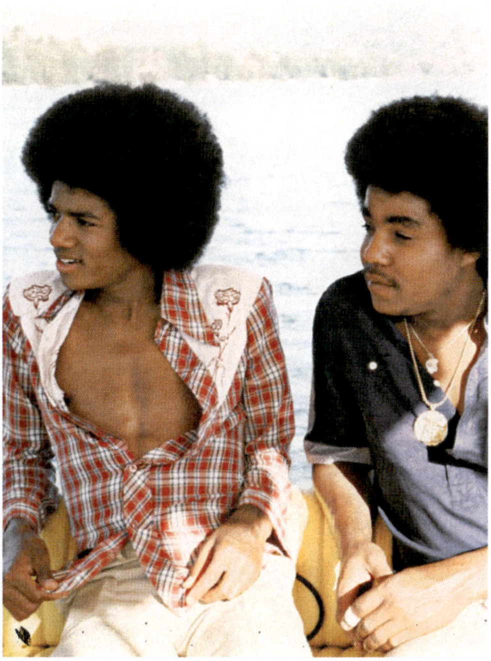

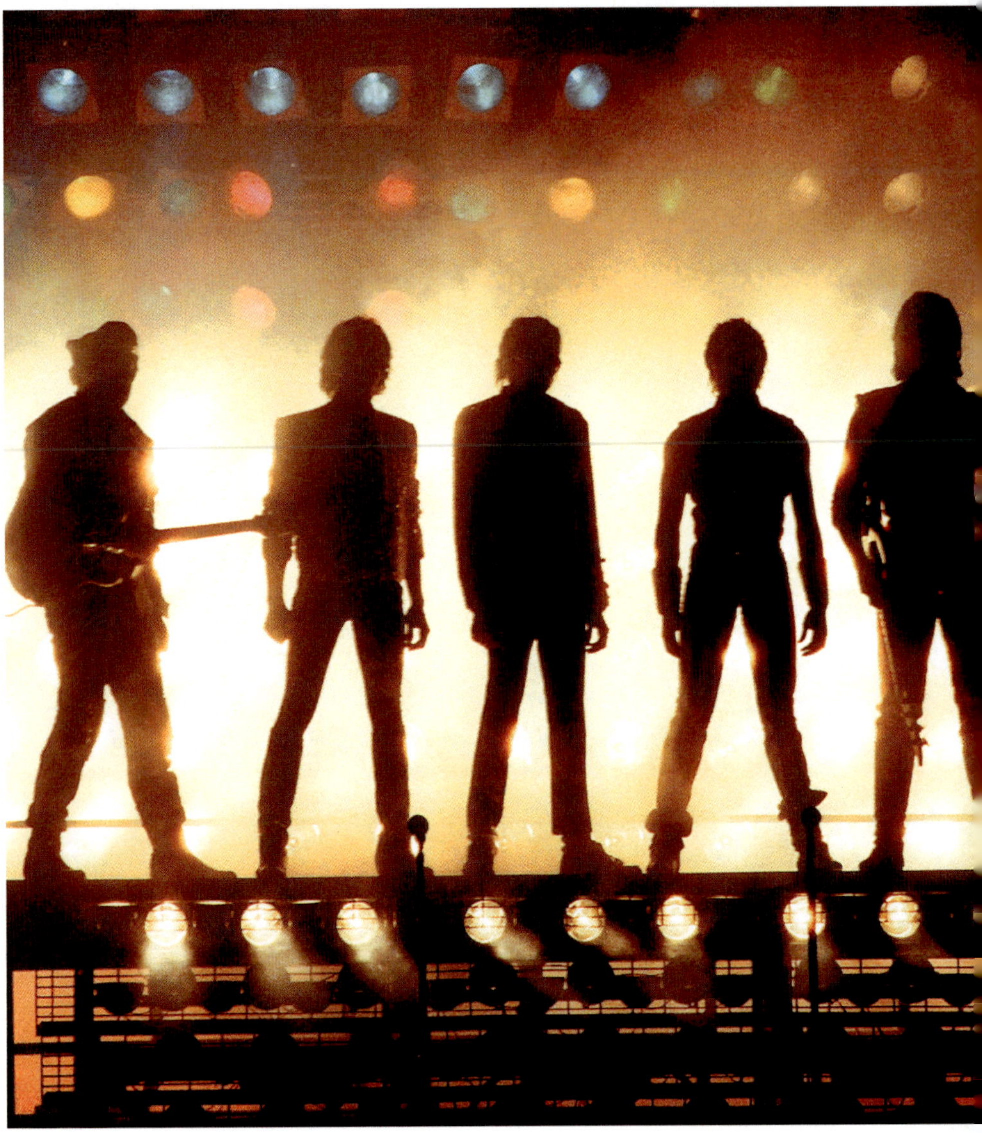

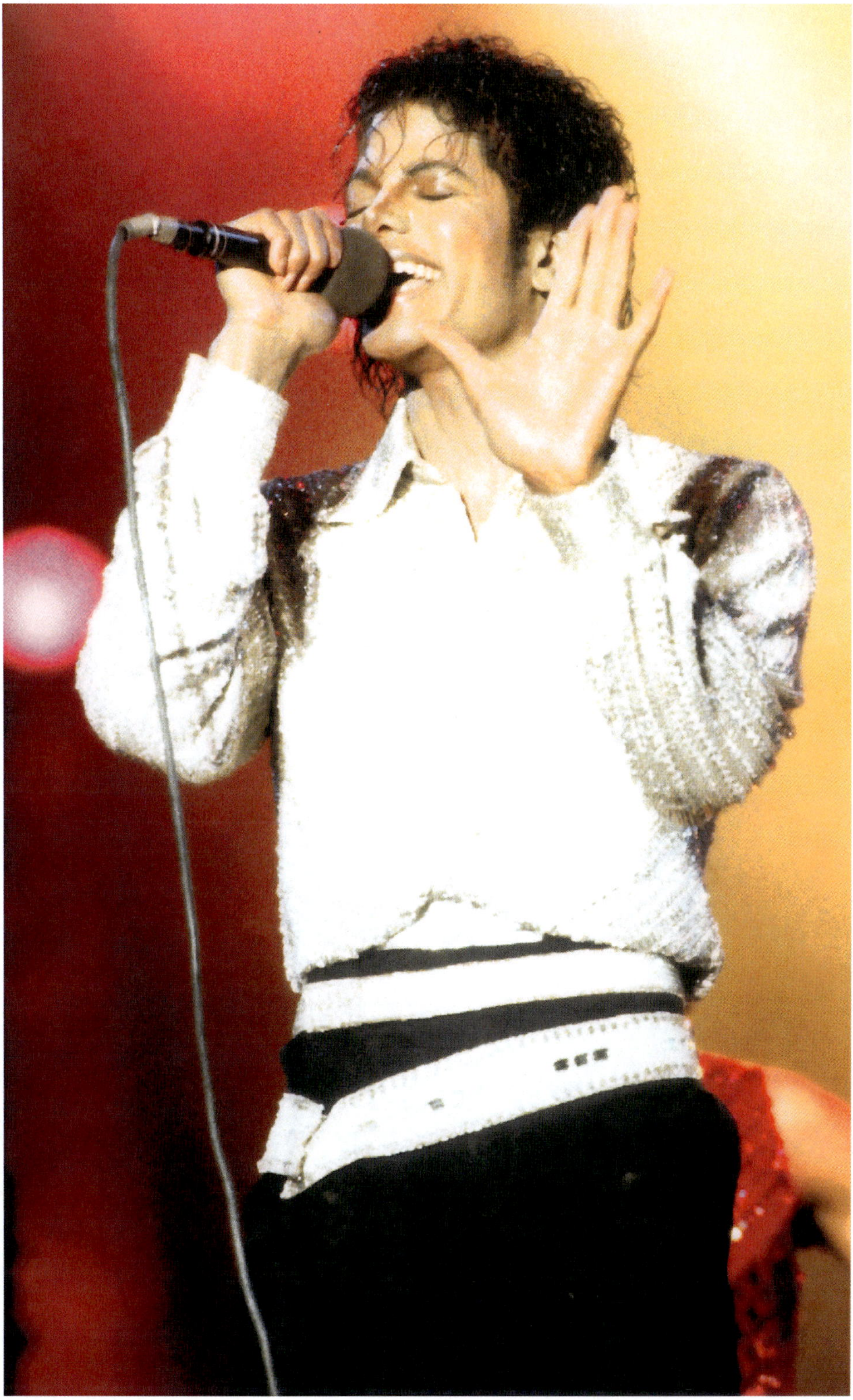

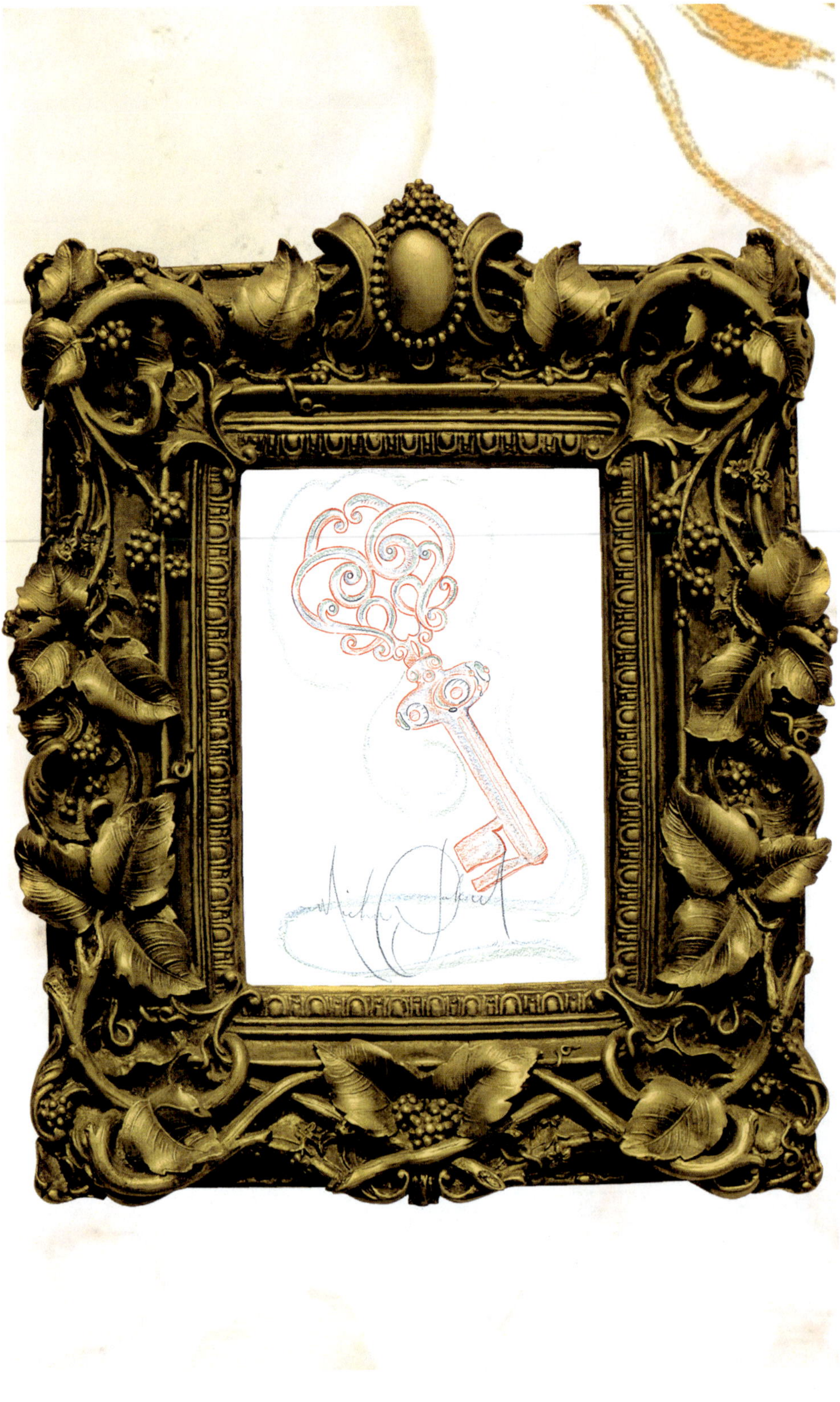

I owe everything to Michael's fans for their unwavering support. No matter what challenges our family faced, the fans were always there for us—through thick and thin. Many of them traveled from across the world just to see Michael, often camping outside our home to catch a glimpse of him.

One moment that truly opened my eyes to Michael's fame occurred on August 29th, his birthday. He took me to Echo Arena in Liverpool, England, where the entire stadium was decorated with balloons and banners that read, "Happy Birthday, Michael." It was a magnificent sight, and I'll never forget it.

The arena was filled with at least 70,000 fans, chanting and screaming, and another 30,000 fans waited outside for a chance to see him. I was both surprised and amazed by the sheer number of people there for my son. It impressed me deeply. In that moment, I realized that something far greater than we could ever have imagined had happened.

Through it all, I was proud that Michael managed to stay grounded. There's no doubt that my son accomplished incredible things in his life, yet he always strived for more, never wanting to rest. This was who he was—everything he did had to be the best. I'm not sure where he got that from. My husband, Joseph, certainly played a role in training the boys for performances. Joseph was strict, which I believe pushed Michael to strive for excellence, especially as the lead singer, with everyone watching him closely.

I know many people were upset with Joseph because he was tough, but I don't believe my husband ever intended to hurt our children. In those days, that was just how we were raised. Joseph did what he felt was best for the boys, and Michael has acknowledged that.

> **When Michael didn't win a grammy for *Off The Wall*, he said, 'Next year, Mother, they won't be able to ignore me.' The following year, he made *Thriller*.**

There are so many moments from Michael's career that made me proud to be his mother. I remember the Grammys in 1983, after the release of Off the Wall. Michael was disappointed that he didn't win any of the awards he had hoped for that year. I was upset too, because I thought the album was great. I recall Michael saying, "Next year, Mother, they won't be able to ignore me."

Then, in 1984, Michael released Thriller. He was nominated for 12 Grammy Awards and won eight—setting a record for the most Grammys ever won by an individual artist in a single year. I know that achievement made him feel better, and he was right—after that, they certainly didn't ignore him.

I knew the sacrifices Michael made from a very young age. He deserved all of his success because he worked tirelessly to achieve it.

Left to Right: Tito, Marlon, Michael, Jackie and Randy.

Left to Right: Marlon, Michael and Randy.

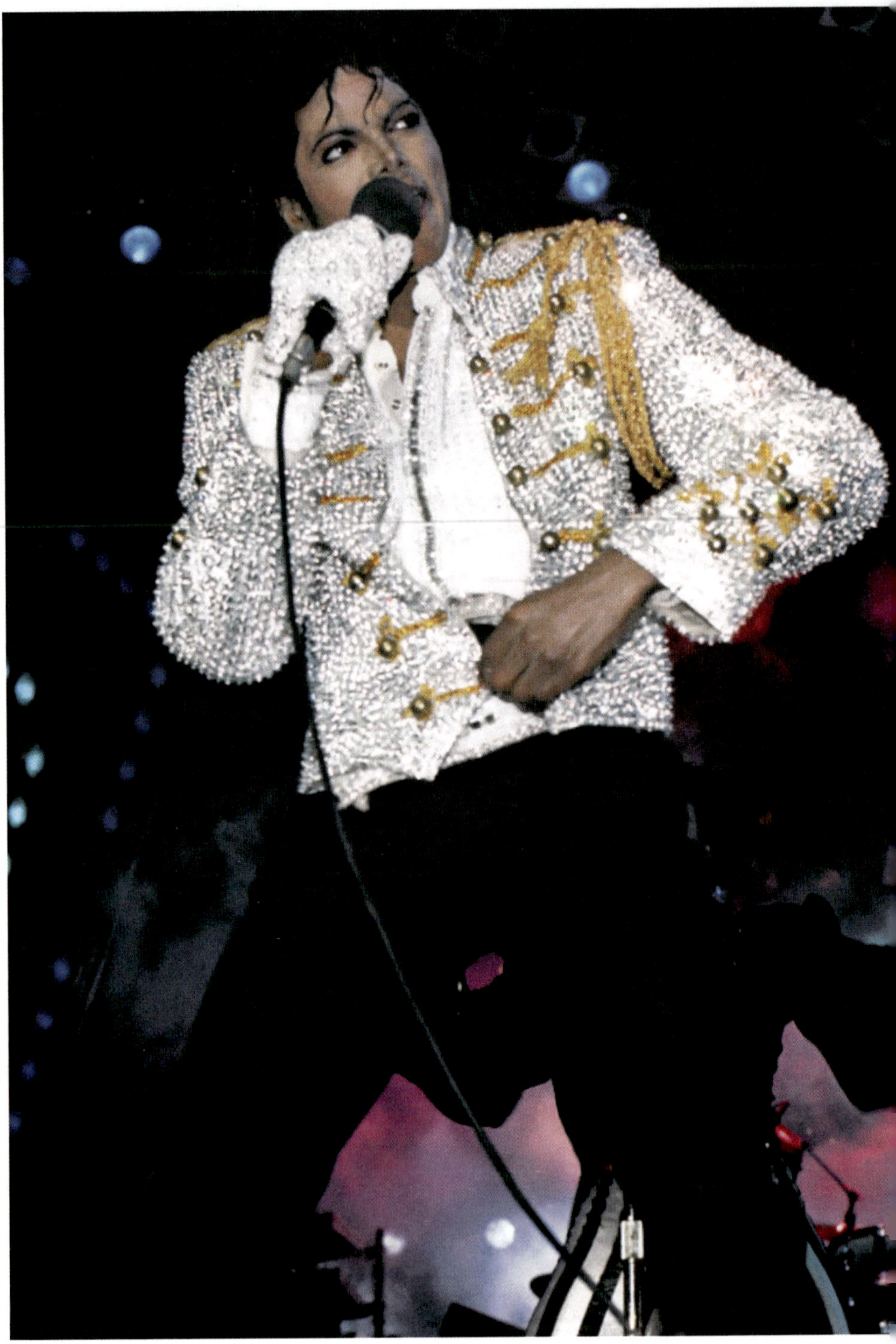

51

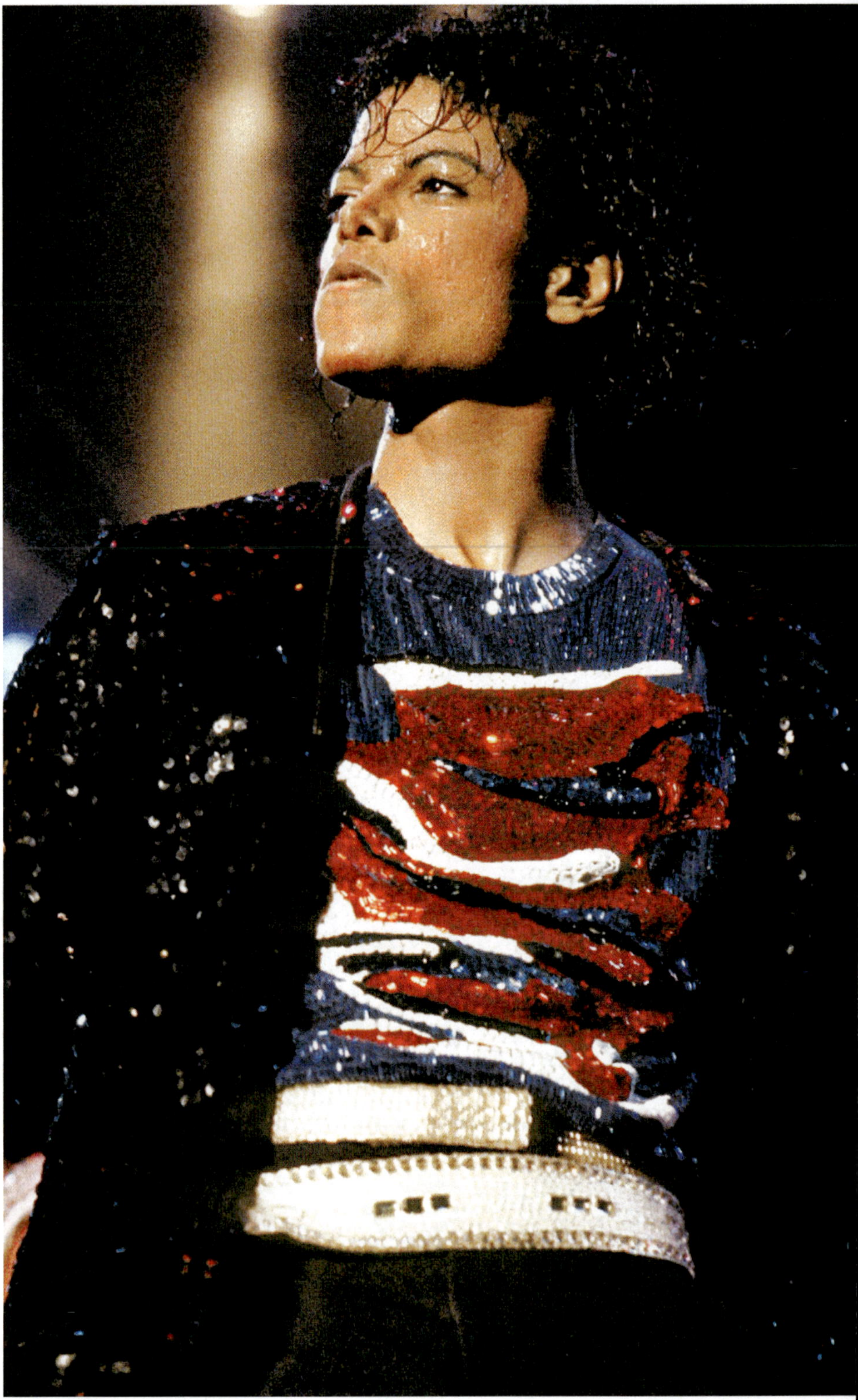

People often ask where Michael learned to dance. He mainly learned by watching TV and picking up moves from his older siblings, Rebbie and Jackie, who were great dancers. He also studied James Brown.

Michael practiced in the studio above our garage, dancing late into the night. He rarely slept. One of my proudest moments was the first time Michael performed the moonwalk during the Motown 25 TV Special. He rehearsed at the house and kept the performance a secret from the family. We didn't know what he was planning, including borrowing my sequinned blazer that he wore for the show.

When he was little, Michael often played basketball with his brothers in the courtyard. He was very competitive and played well since he could move quickly. As a teenager, he decided to become a vegetarian, both for health reasons and to help reduce the acne he struggled with during that time. It made me sad to see Michael unhappy with his appearance.

Michael practiced dancing every Sunday, it was singing with choreography to train his voice. Though he had some training, he was just a natural. He believed in hard work and always thanked God for his success.

> **One of my proudest moments was the first time Michael performed the moonwalk during Motown 25.**

Michael's greatest influences were Fred Astaire and James Brown. He was also inspired by the Temptations, Jackie Wilson, and Elvis Presley. We were fortunate to meet Elvis in Las Vegas in the early 70s, and he treated us really well. At the time, Michael hadn't yet reached fame, so it was an unforgettable moment for all of us.

I remember when my boys opened for James Brown; he was initially upset to be performing with a children's act, fearing they might steal the show, as children do. Eventually, Mr. Brown got past it and Michael became very close.

When people ask about my favorite songs from Michael's solo albums, I often say *"Man in the Mirror"* (1988) and *"Earth Song"* (1995). I also love the Jackson Five hit *"Man of War,"* which has the lyrics: *"Man of war, don't go to war no more, study peace, because peace is what we need."*

I have to admit, I'm proud of Michael's solo albums, but I still prefer when he performed with his brothers, as the group.

I often told Michael that before I leave this earth, I would love to see *The Jacksons* back together. Michael promised me that it would eventually happen, but sadly, I never got to see that day.

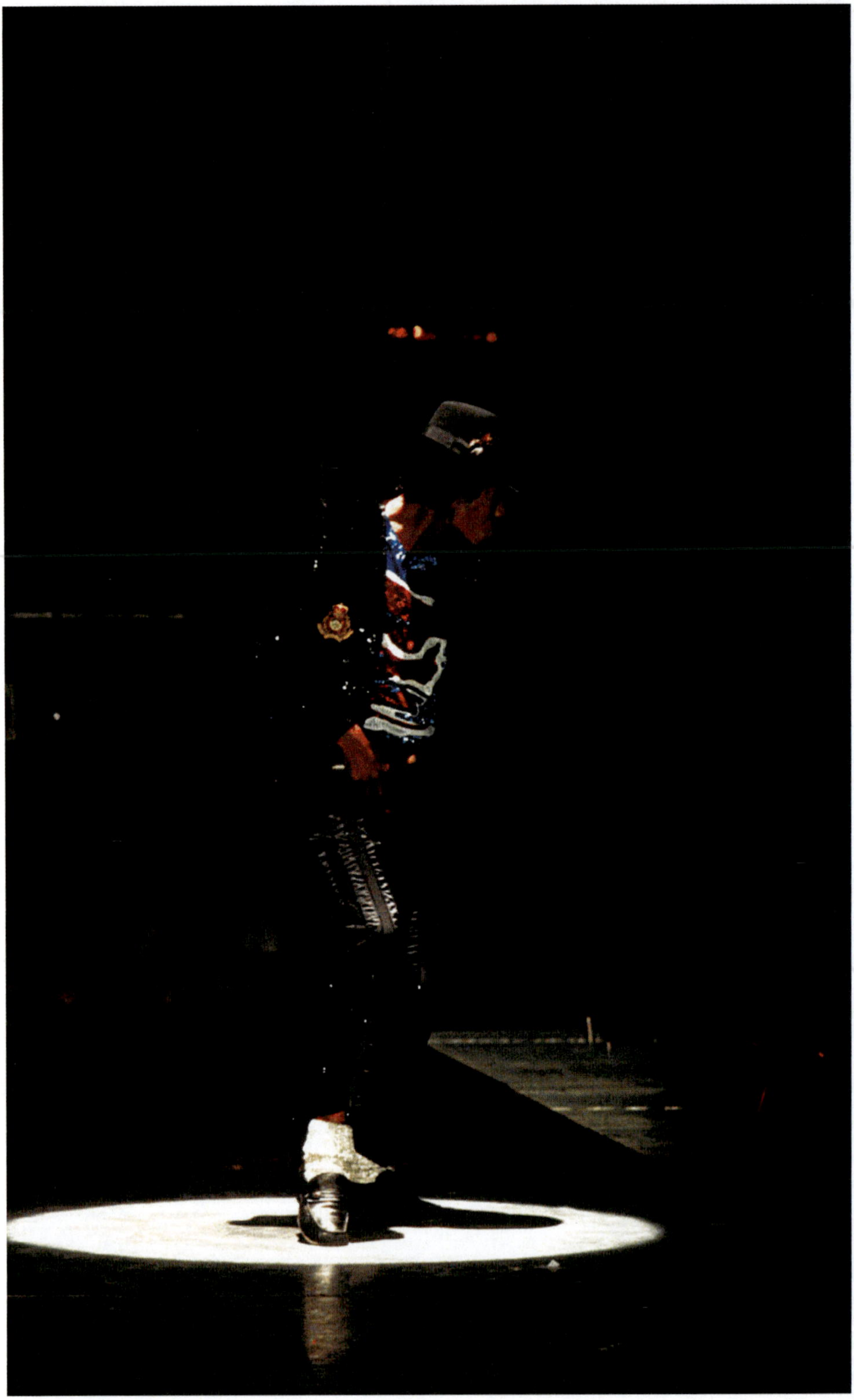

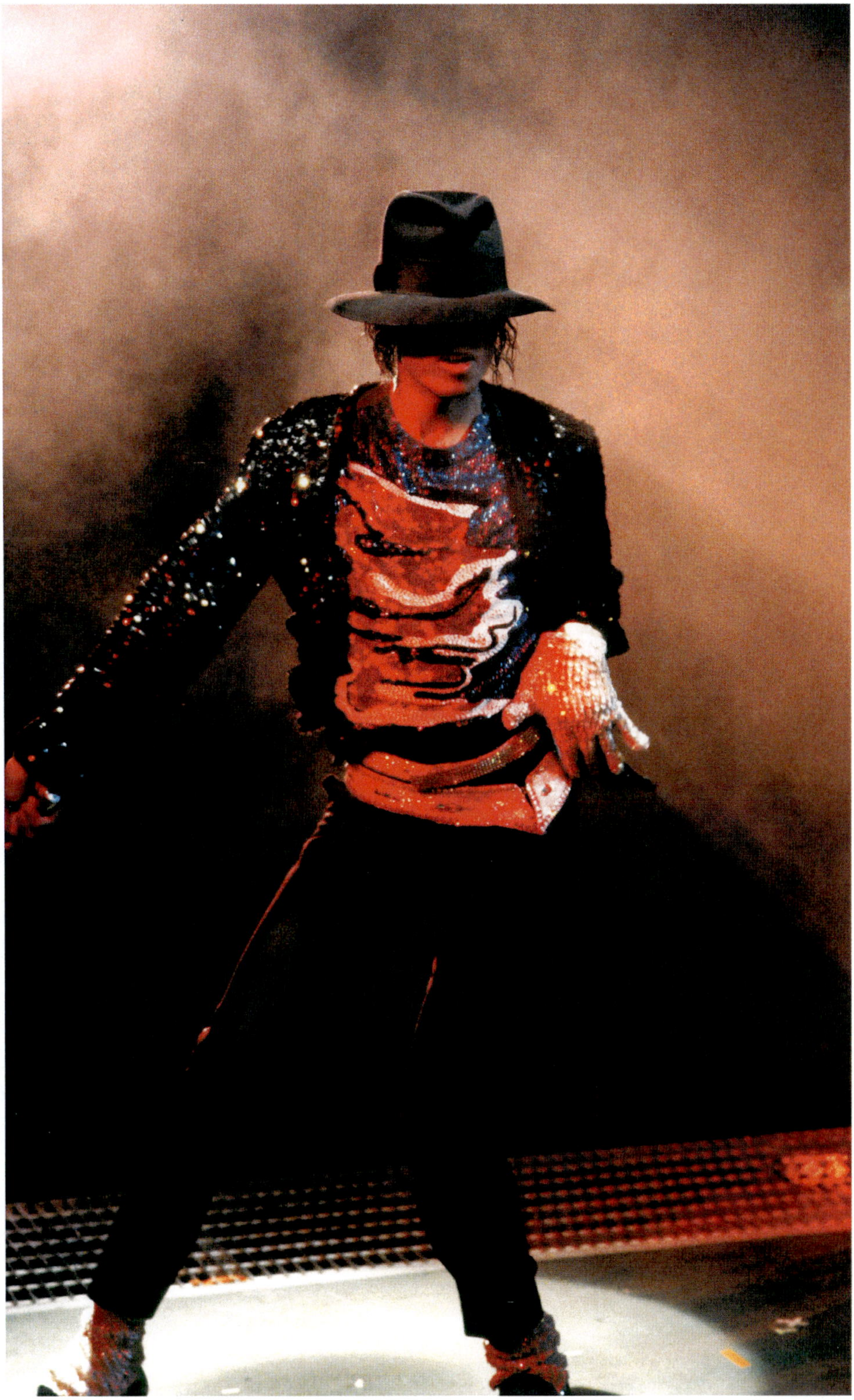

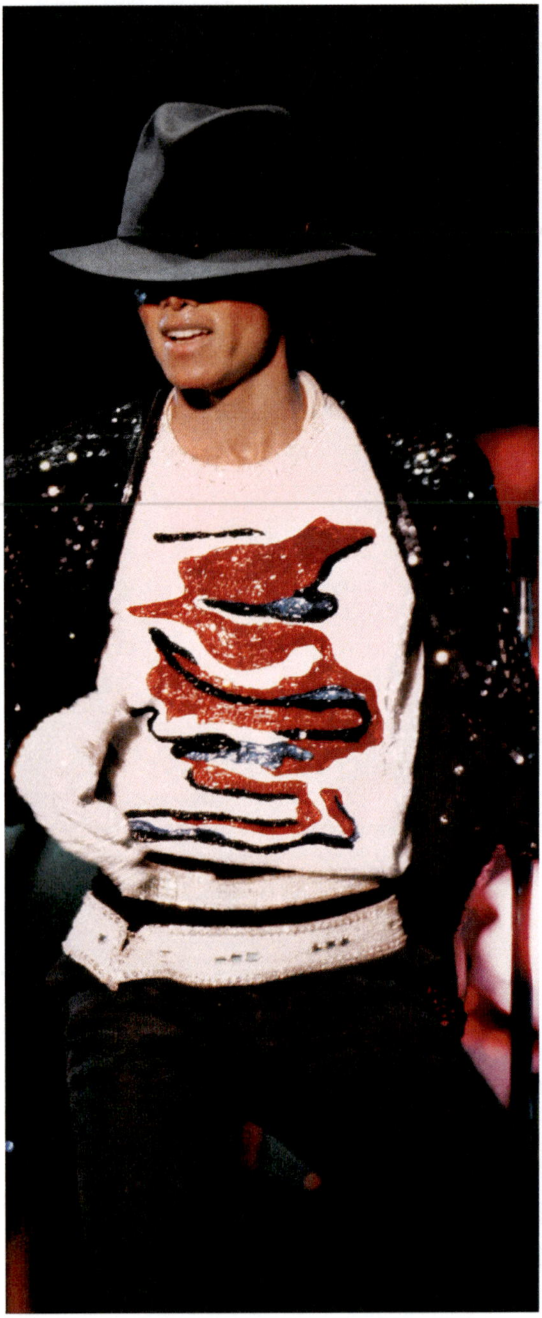
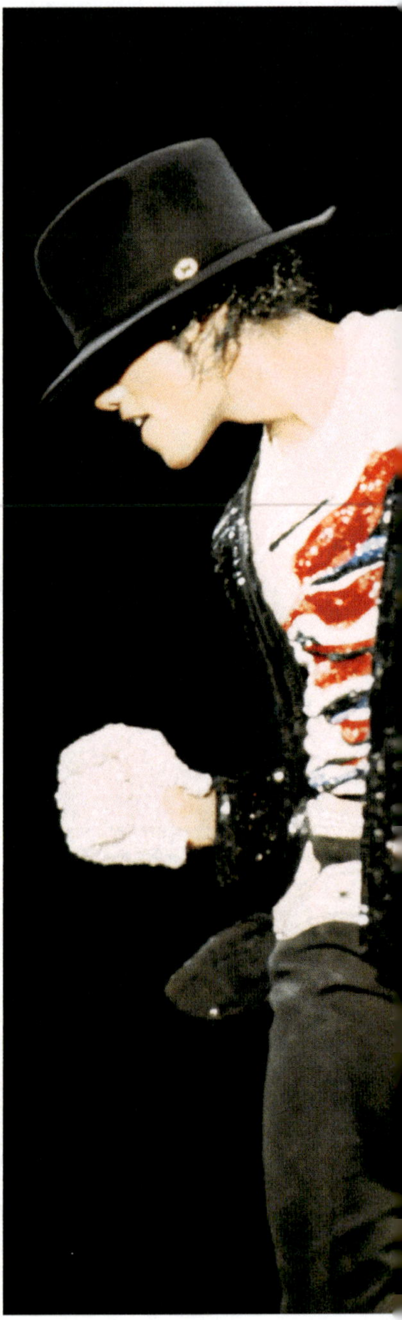

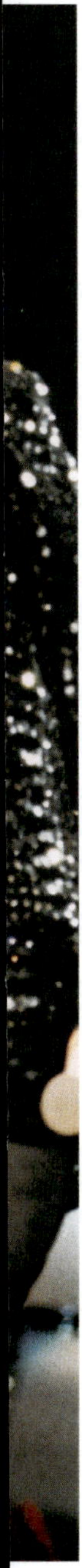
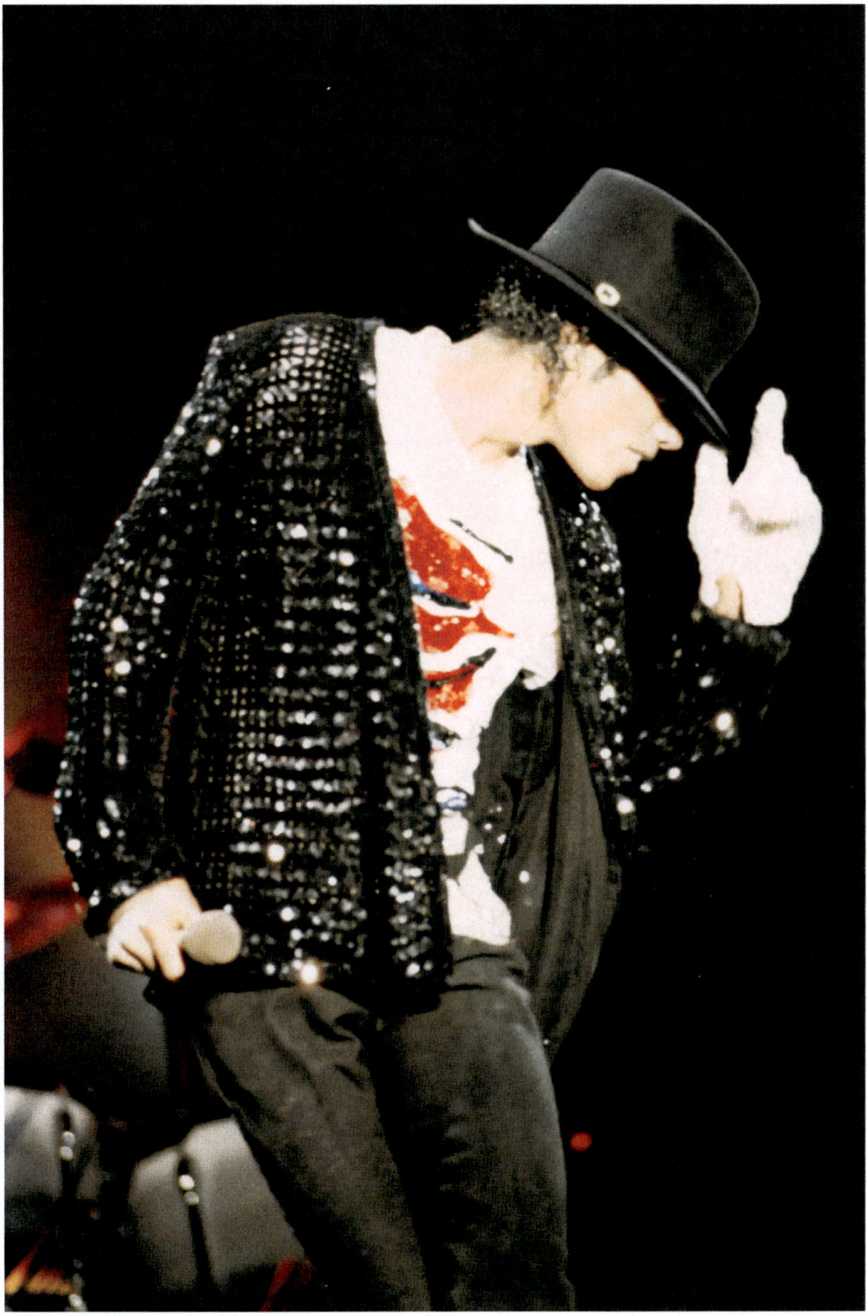

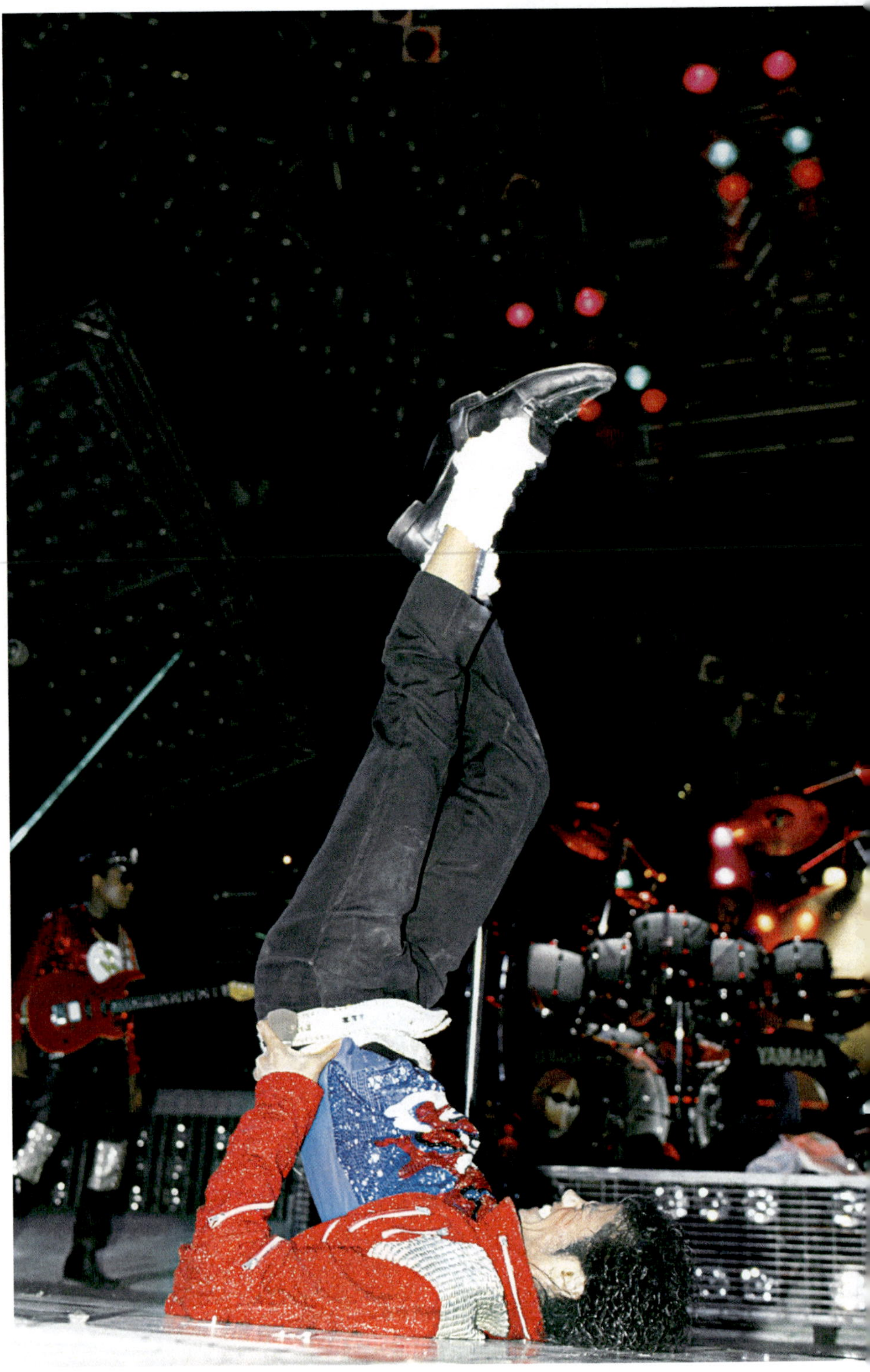
YAMAHA

Performing meant everything to Michael. Working on the family's variety show turned Michael's interests toward acting, which later evolved into his love for Broadway after working on The Wiz with Diana Ross and Quincy Jones. Michael once shared that he loved the escapism that acting provided him—he loved the idea of forgetting who he was and imagining life through someone else's eyes.

This love for theater began to influence Michael's music, especially in his videos, or "short films," as he called them—because they were inspired by his passion for movies. He had a natural gift for telling stories through the lens of different characters. He loved fantasy and magic and enjoyed putting on a show that would have people on the edge of their seats.

Most people don't realize that Michael was involved in more than just performing music. He wrote many songs for other people's albums in the 80's.

For example, Michael wrote Diana Ross's 1982 hit "Muscles" and Rebbie's 1984 song "Centipede." He also co-wrote "We Are the World" with Lionel Richie in 1985. He provided backing vocals for The Doobie Brothers' hit "What a Fool Believes" and sang the chorus on Rockwell's "Somebody's Watching Me."

Michael composed the backbeat for songs like "Billie Jean" and "Don't Stop 'Til You Get Enough." He told me that "Heal the World" and "Will You Be There" were his favorite songs to write, as they shared his messages of peace, love, and goodwill.

> **Michael loved acting— he loved the idea of forgetting who he was and experiencing life through someone else's eyes**

Just like singing and dancing were natural for Michael, so was writing music and composing sounds. Sometimes, Michael could write an entire song overnight. He didn't sleep whenever inspiration would strike. I often heard him in his room, up all night working on his music, and he wouldn't rest until he felt satisfied with his work.

Michael's motivation stayed with him throughout his entire life. He loved working, he loved creating, and he was involved in every kind of entertainment, even if it was behind the scenes.

One dream Michael never had the chance to accomplish was becoming a movie director. Making movies is something I wish Michael could have pursued, because he was so passionate about it. Michael studied by shadowing great filmmakers like Francis Ford Coppola and Steven Spielberg, both of whom were dear friends of his, and both of whom also recognized his potential to become one of the great directors himself. Unfortunately, Michael's music career was too demanding at the time for him to focus on directing movies, but I know he planned to do it after his final This Is It tour.

During the 1990s, Michael was involved in some interesting negotiations; he wanted to buy Marvel Superhero Films long before they became a huge trend, and he even tried purchasing the company so he could play a character like Spider-Man.

Sadly, Michael didn't fulfill his dreams of making films, but many of his other dreams did happen.

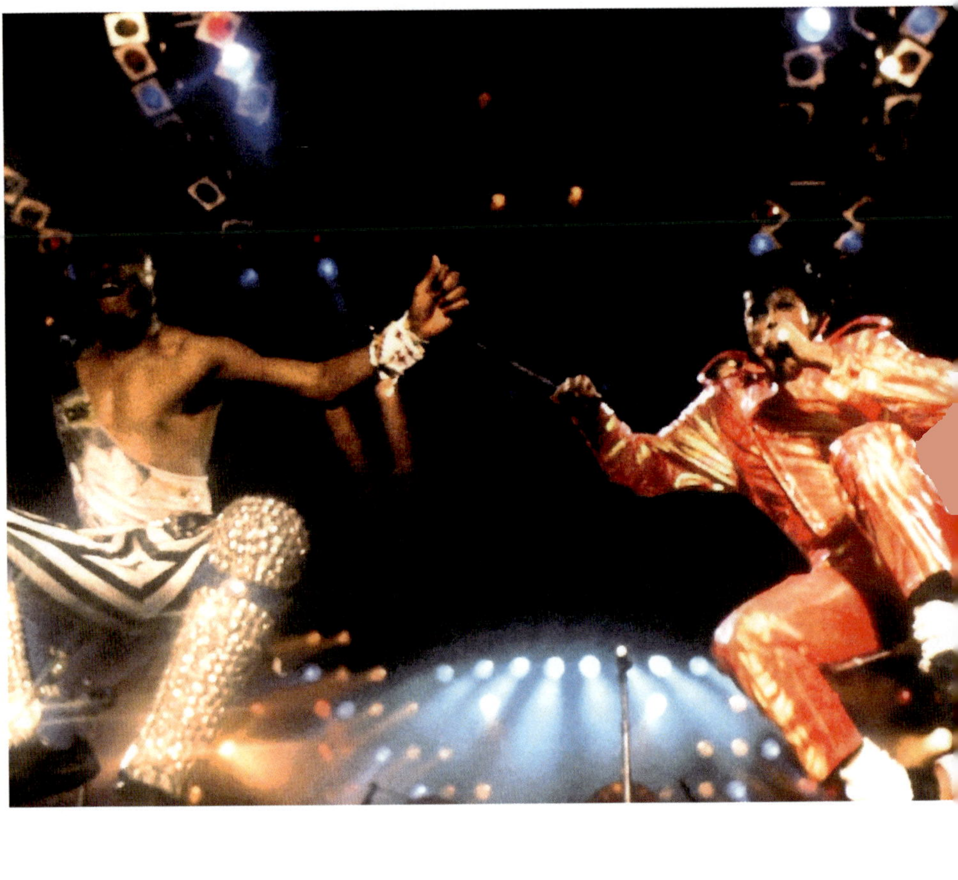

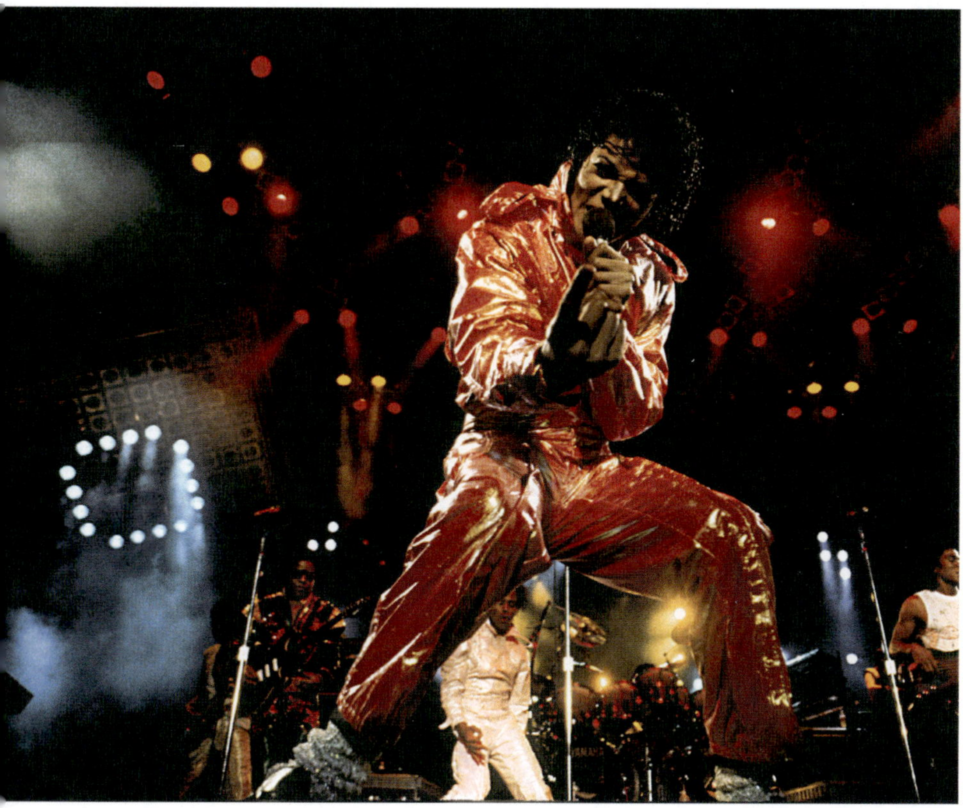

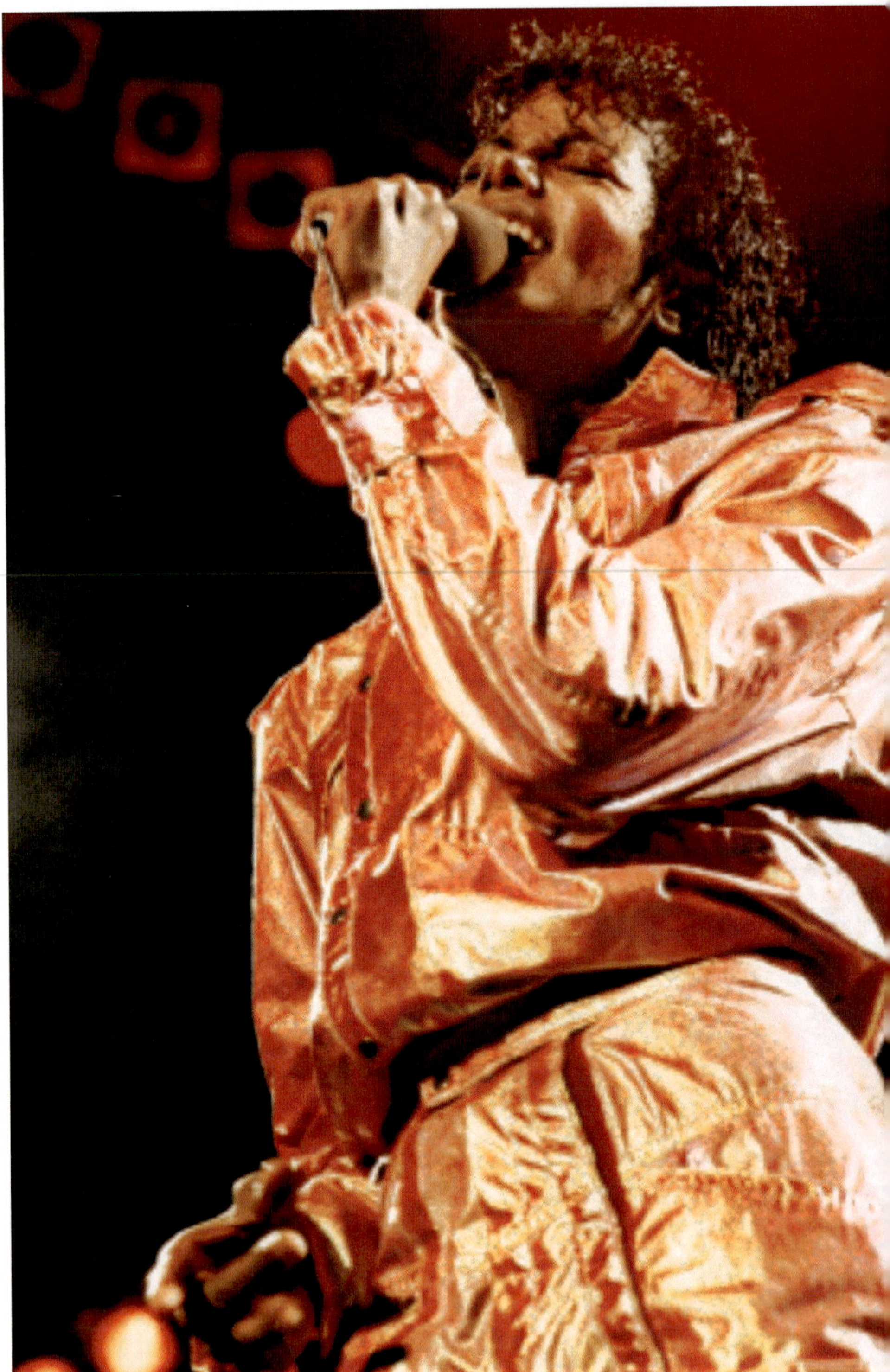

63

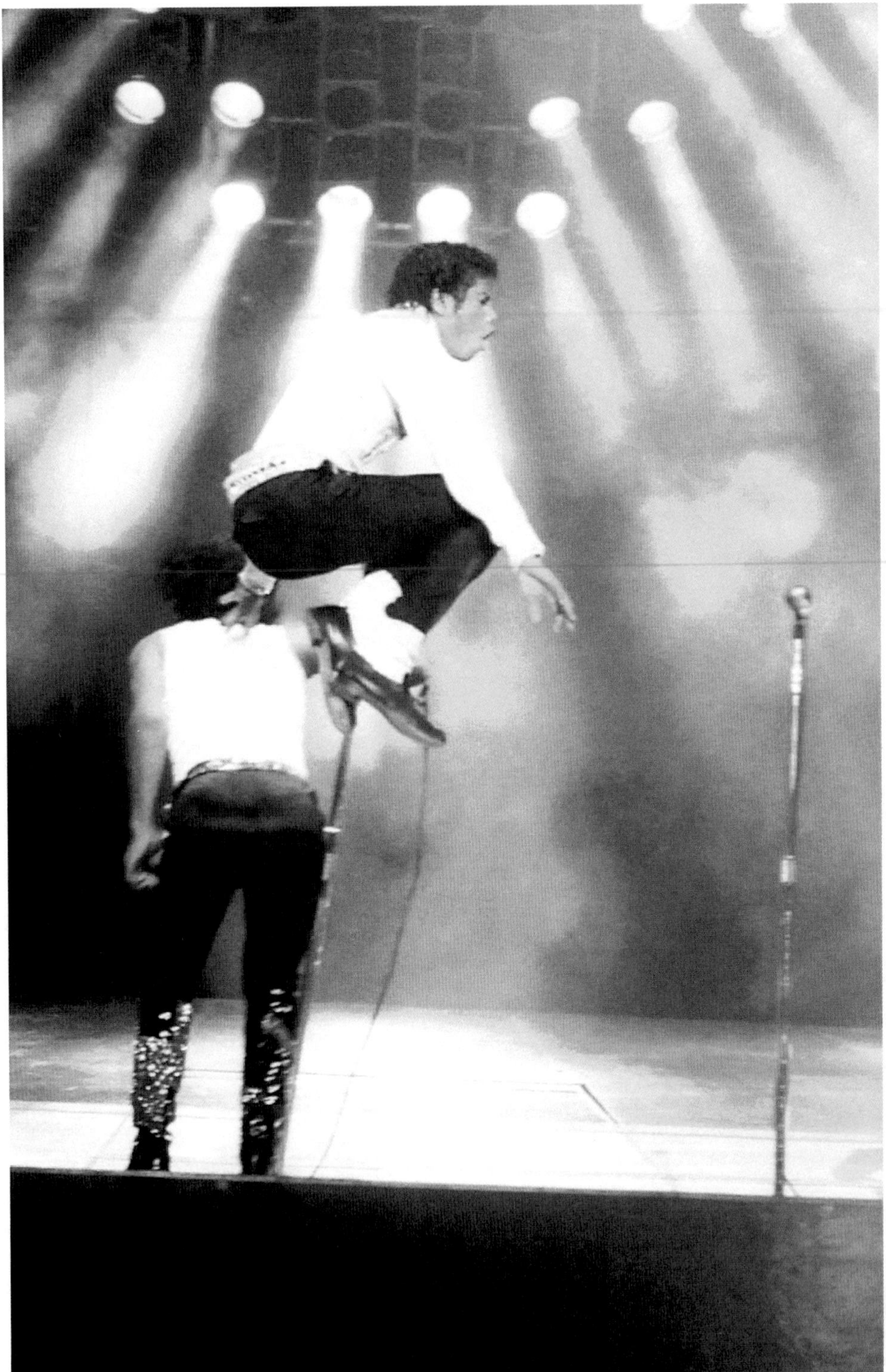

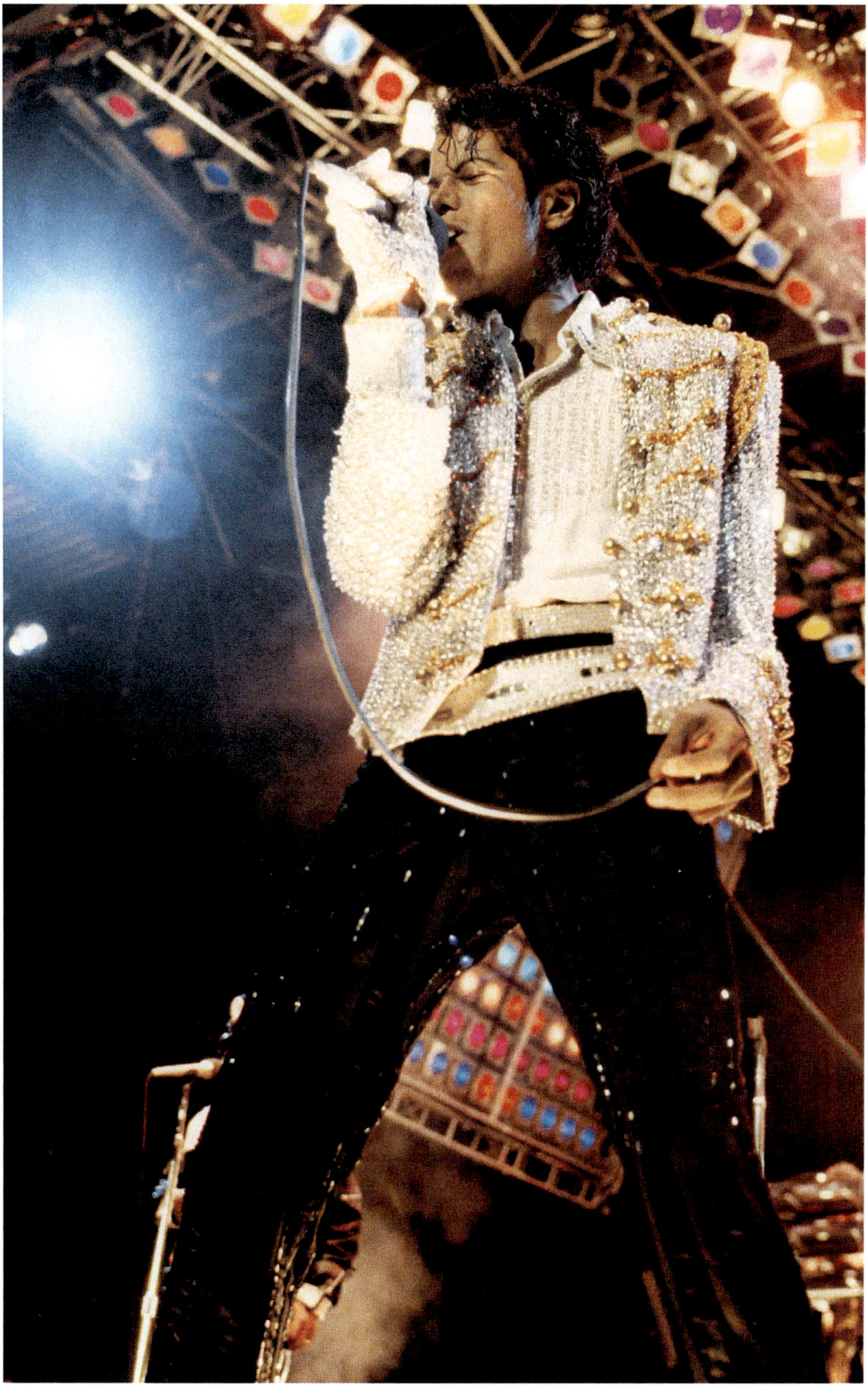

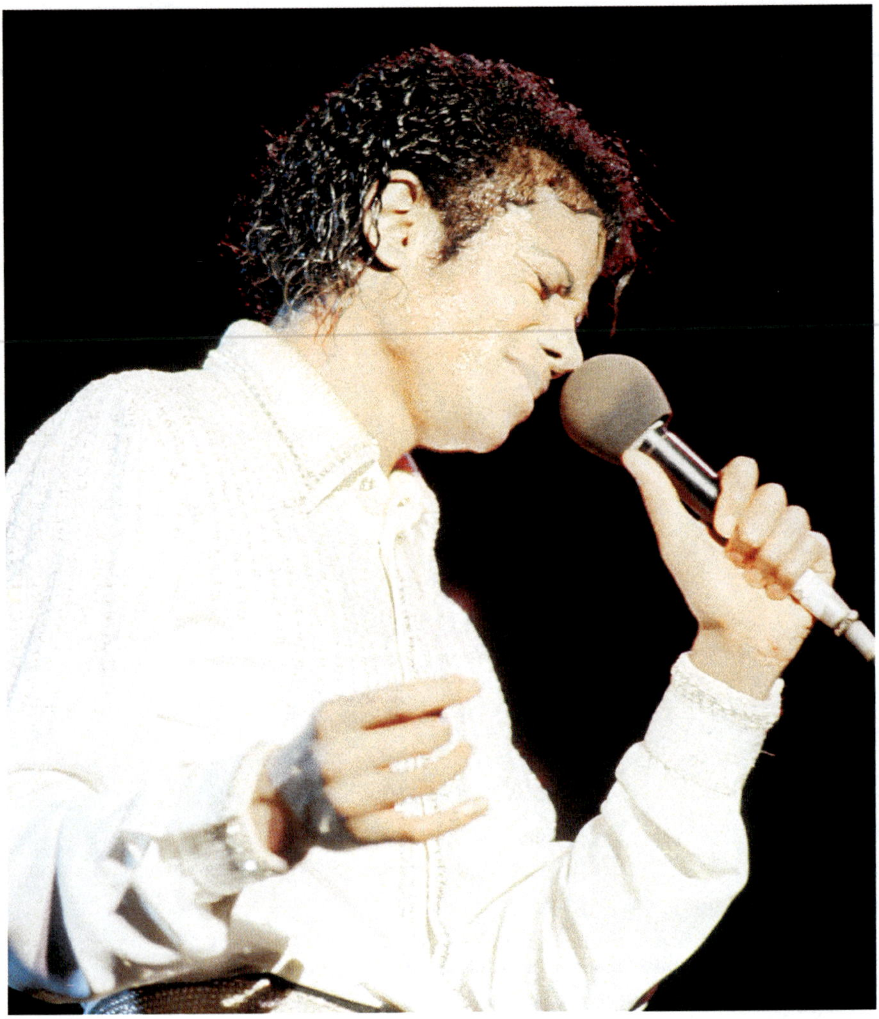

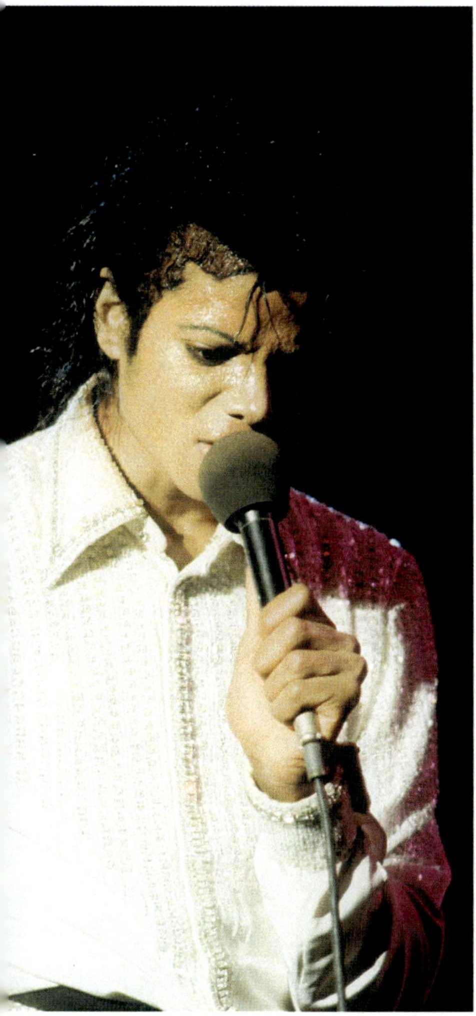
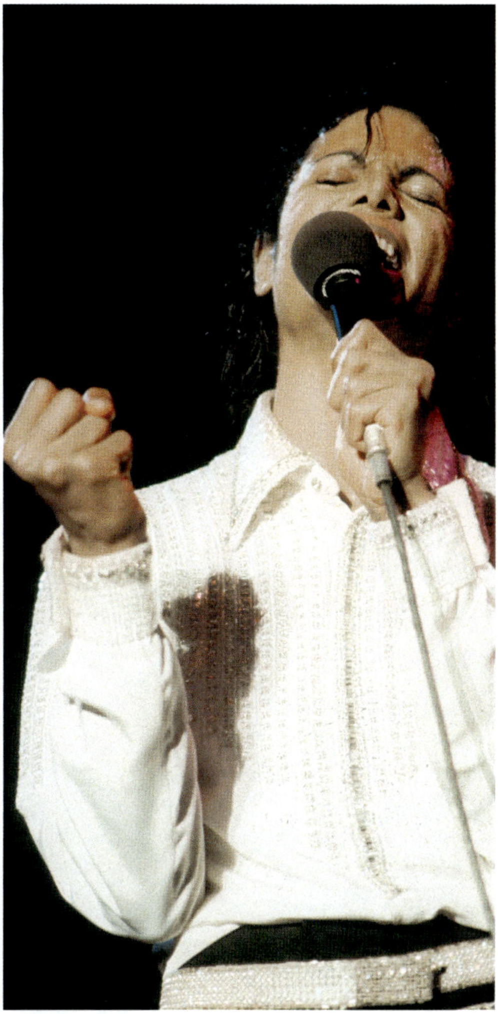

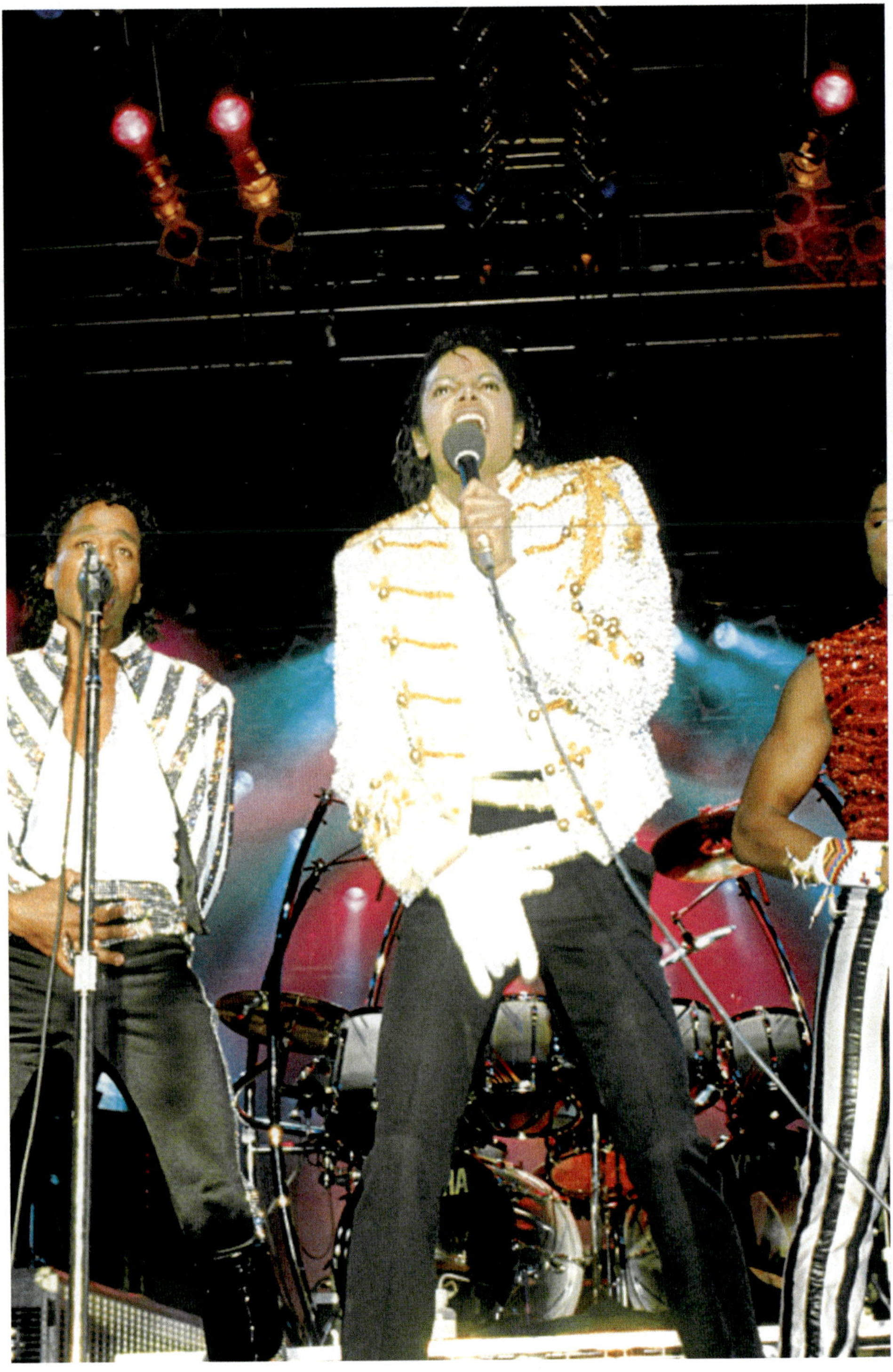

69

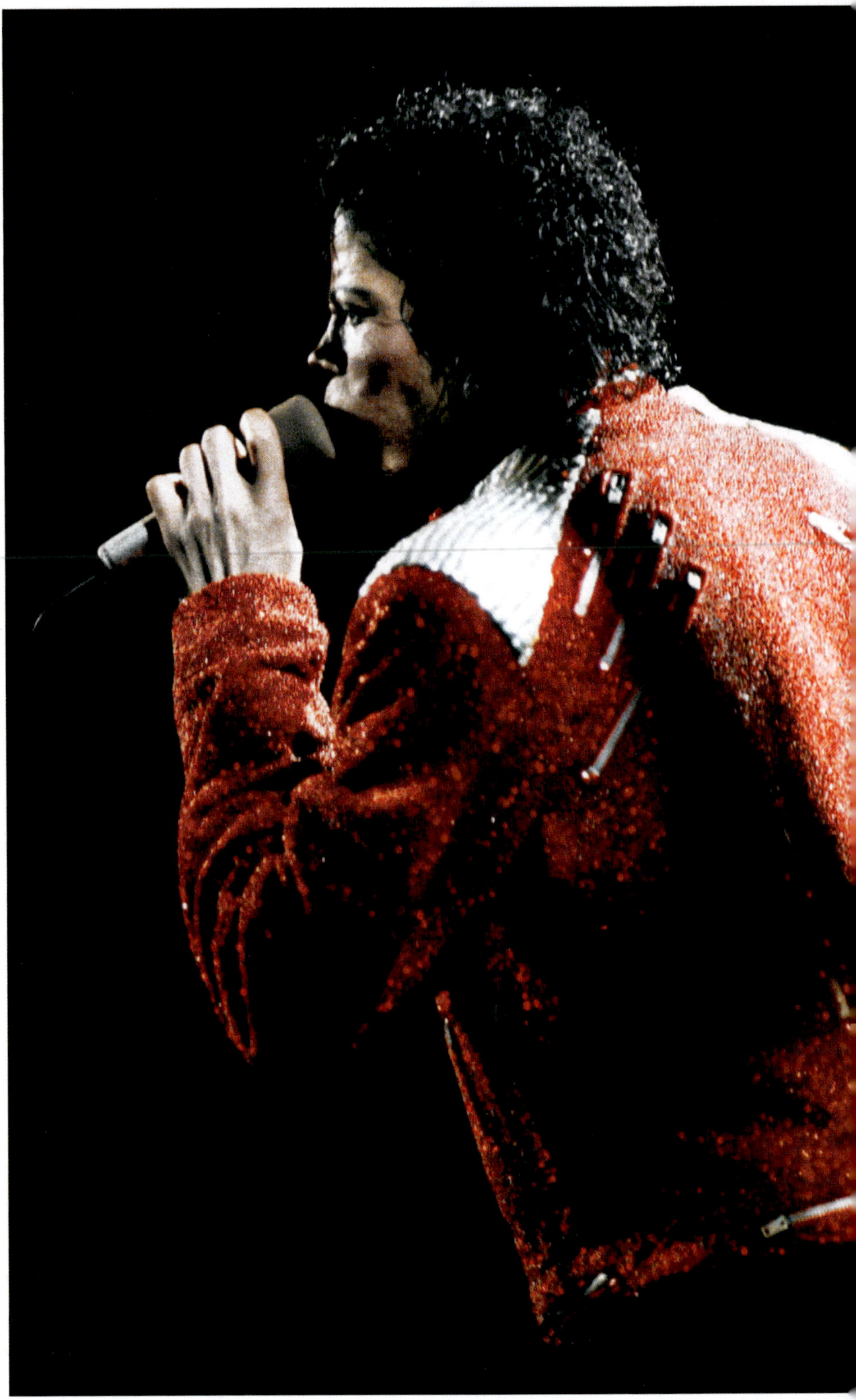

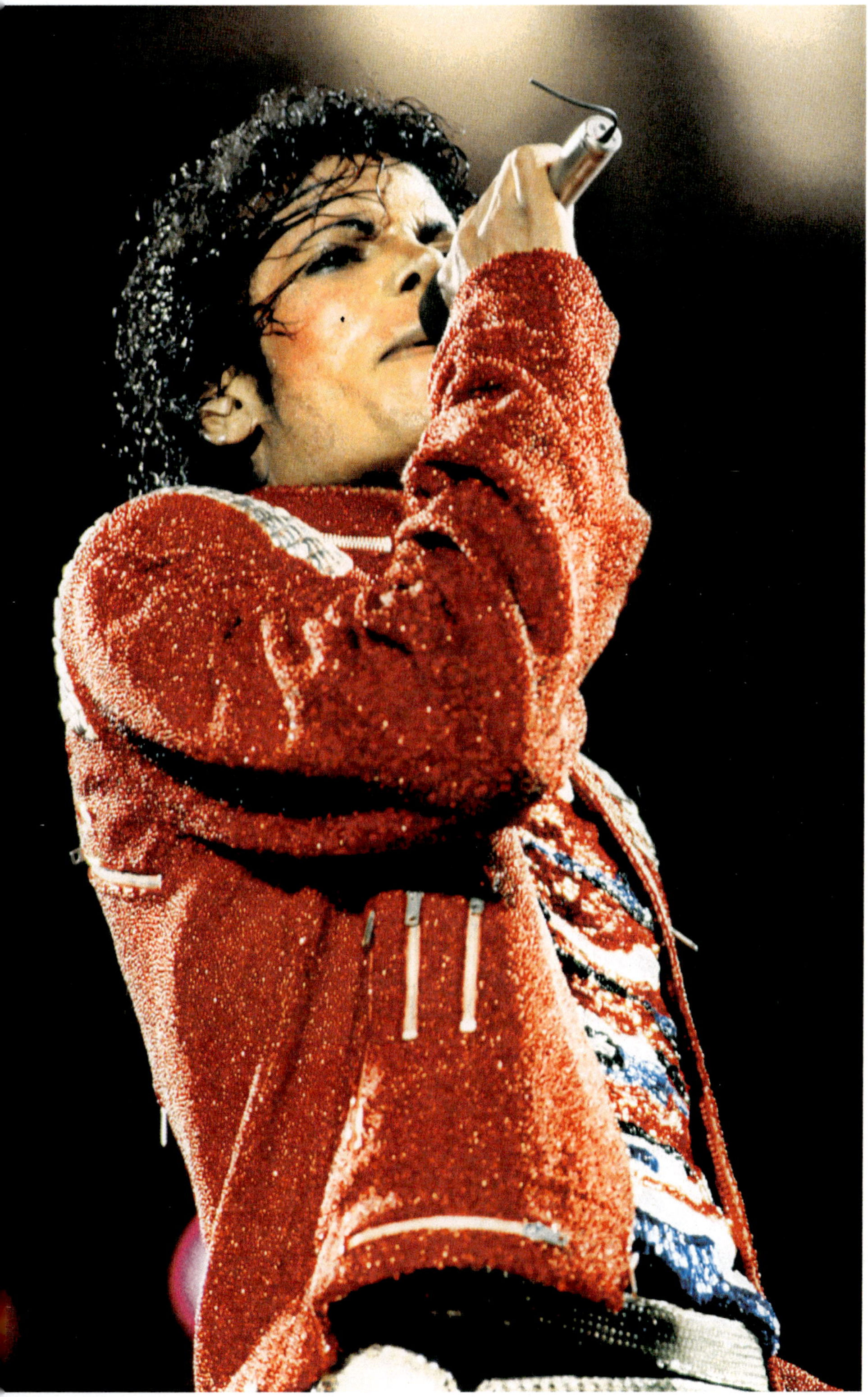

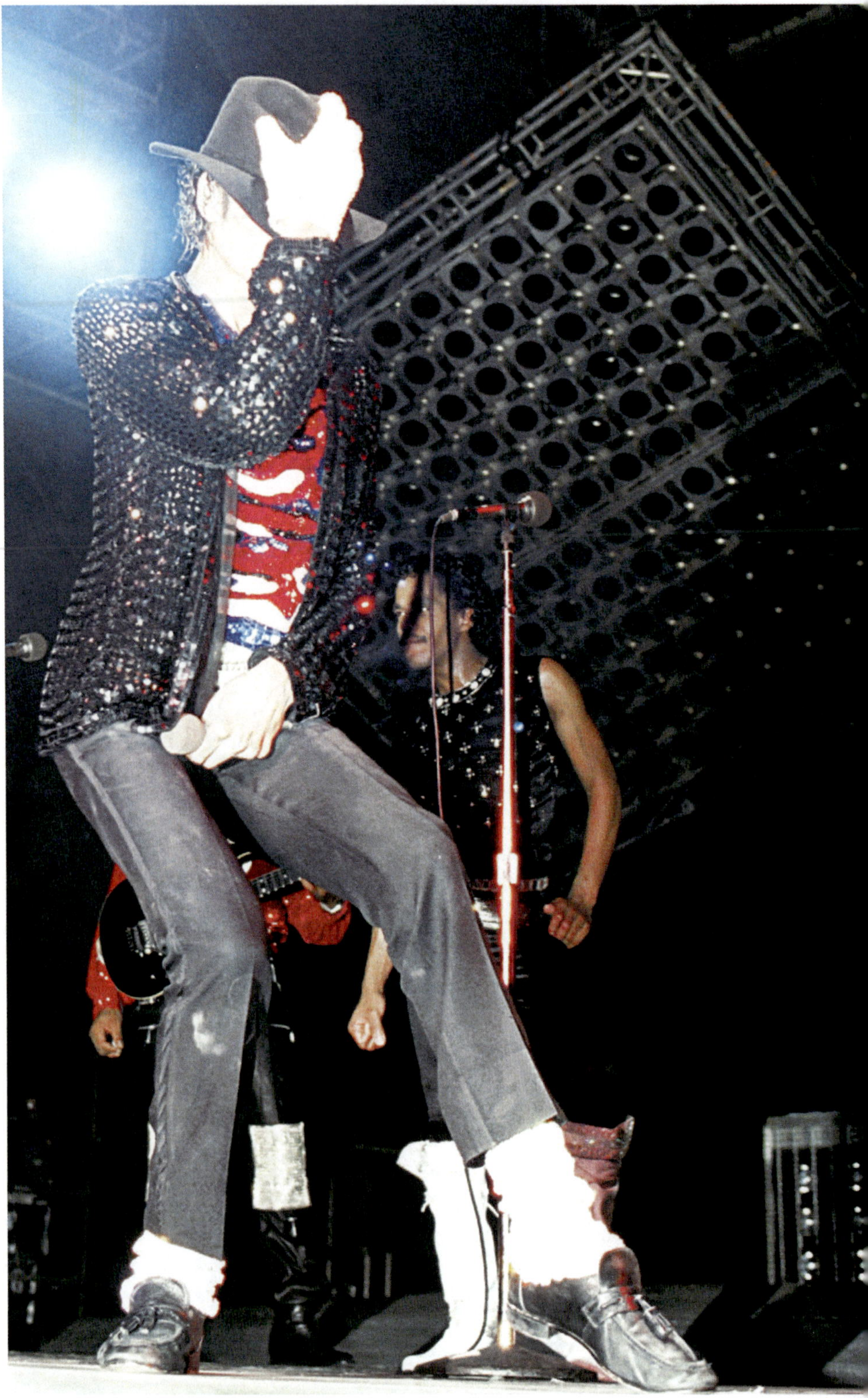

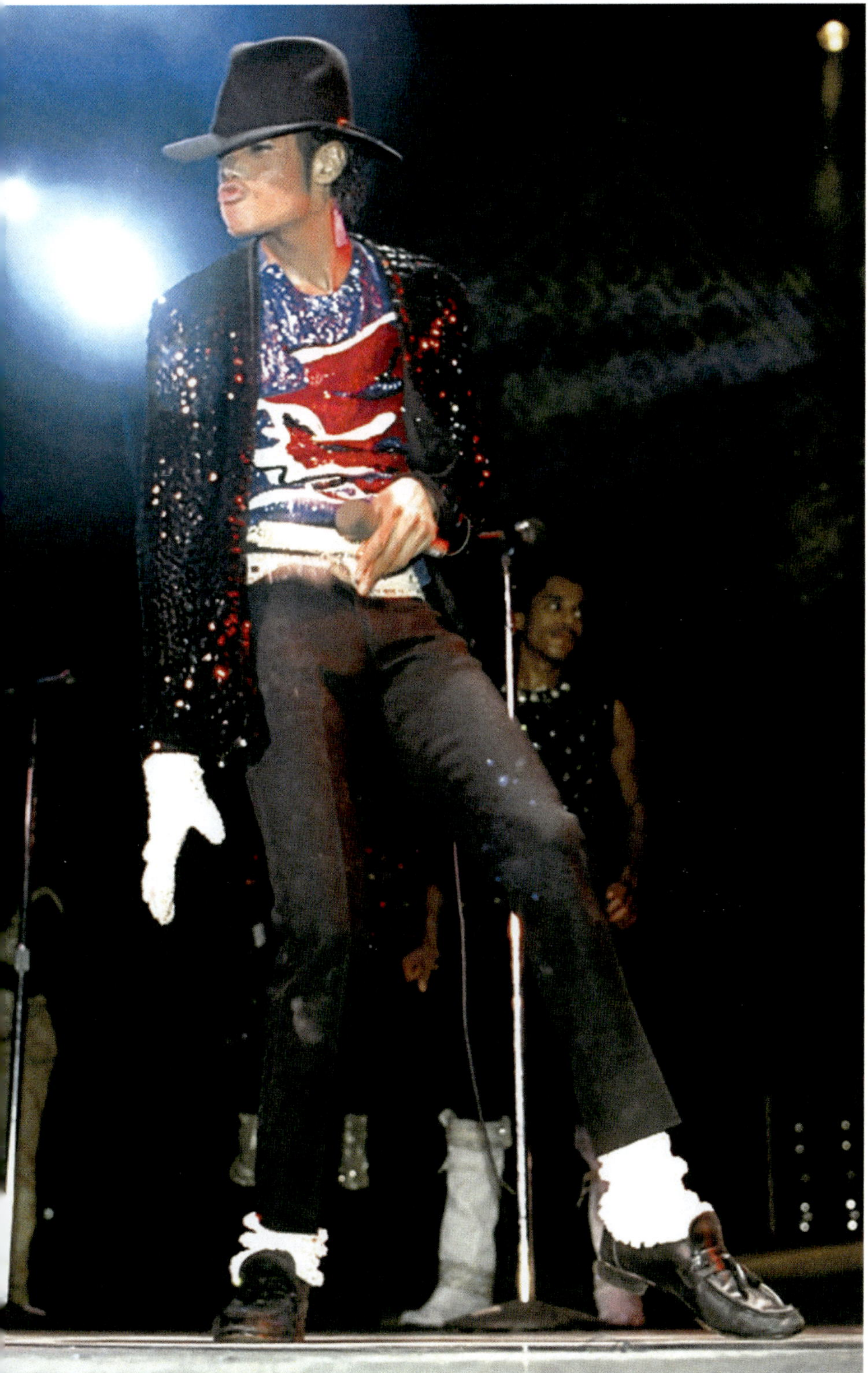

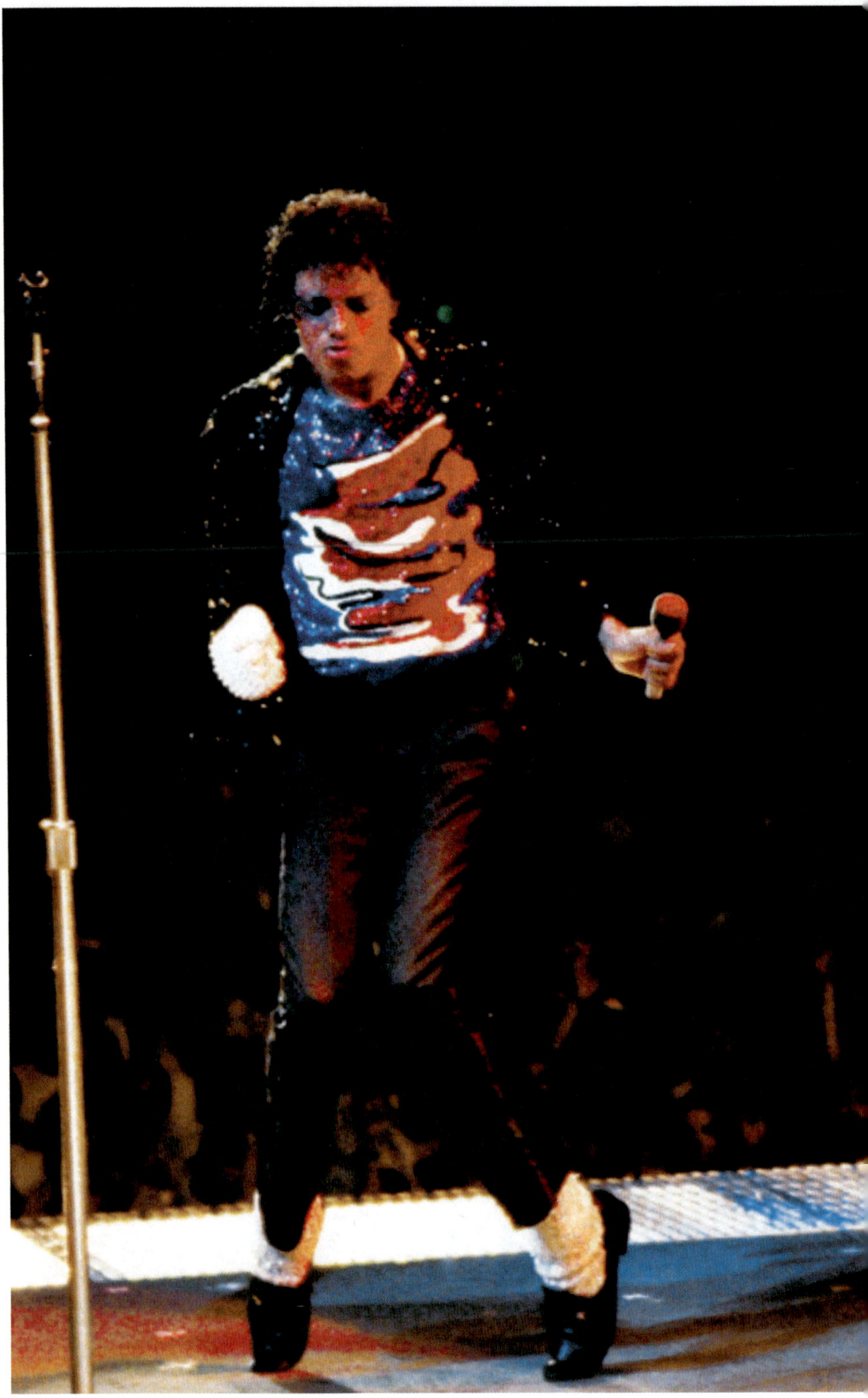

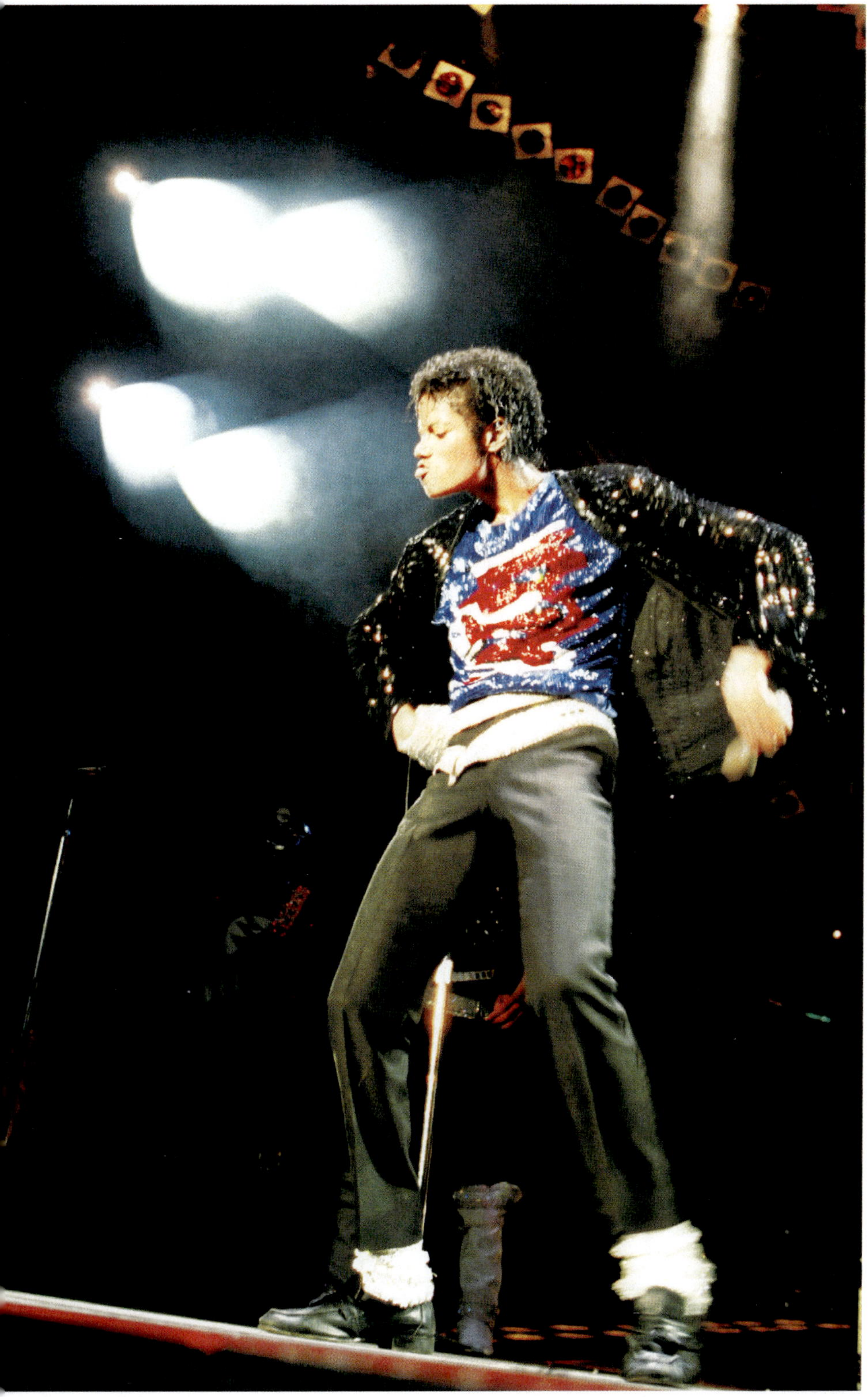

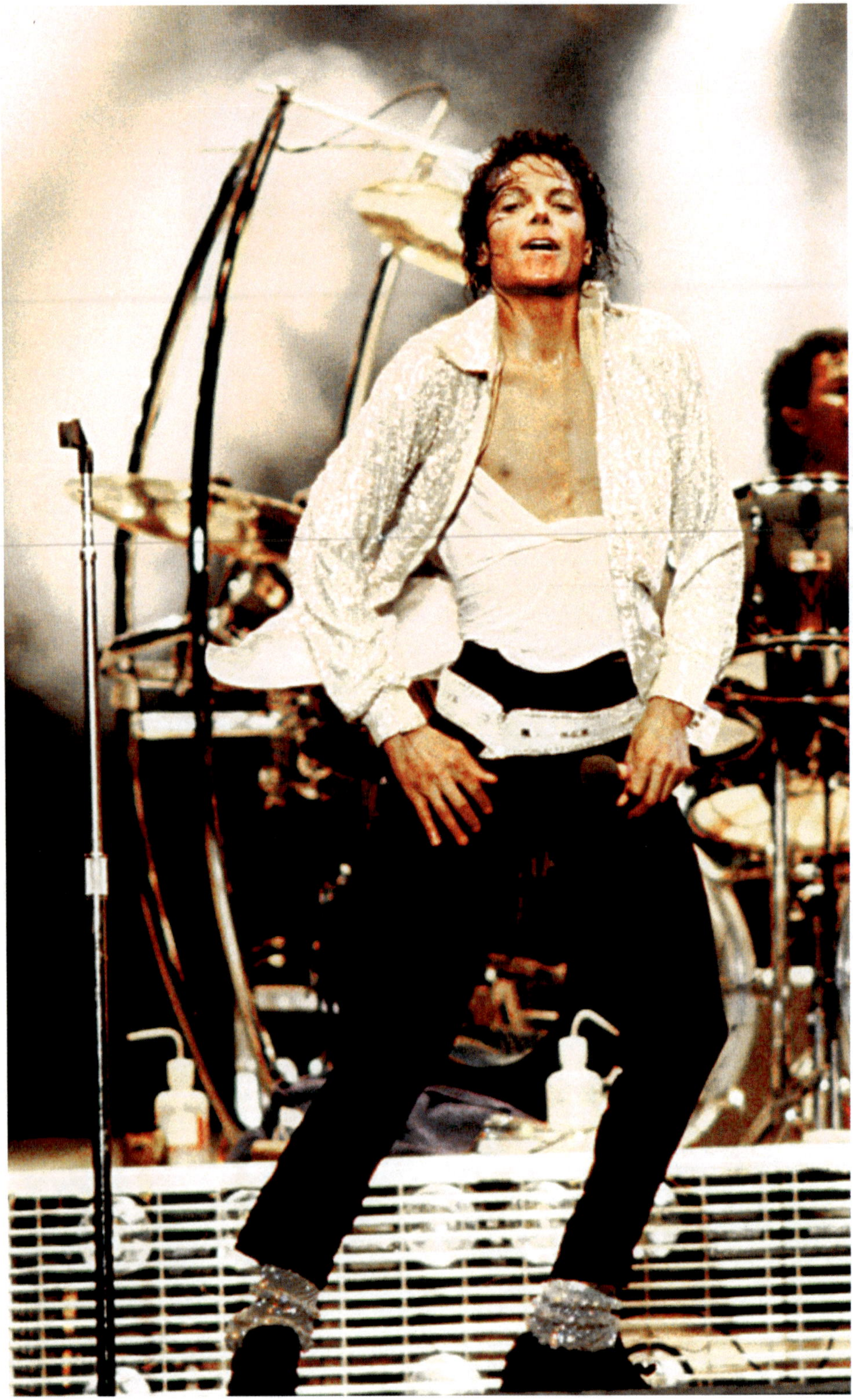

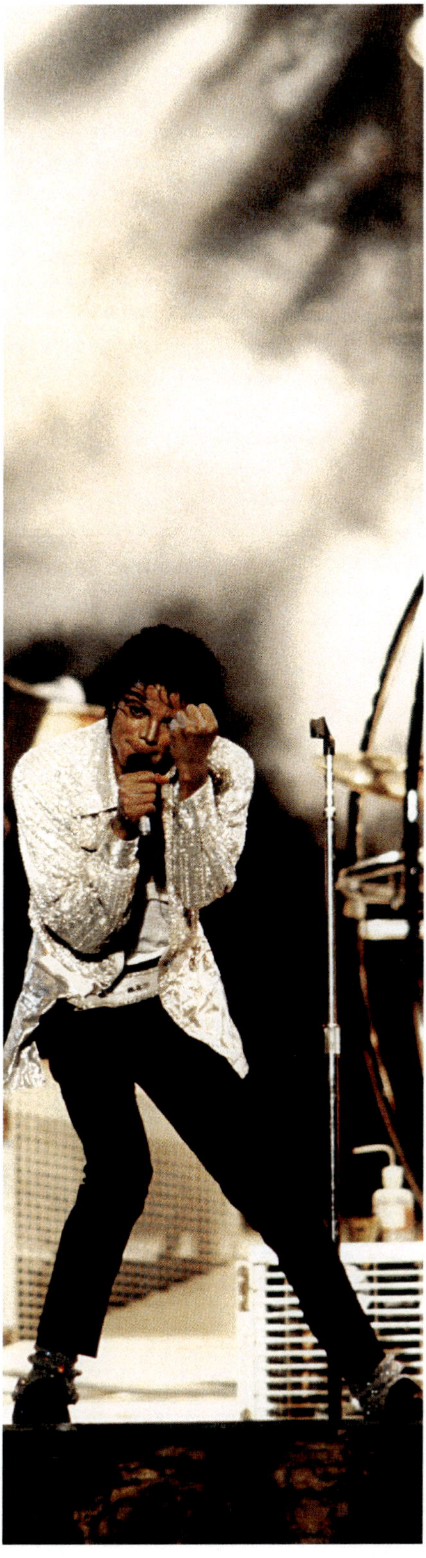
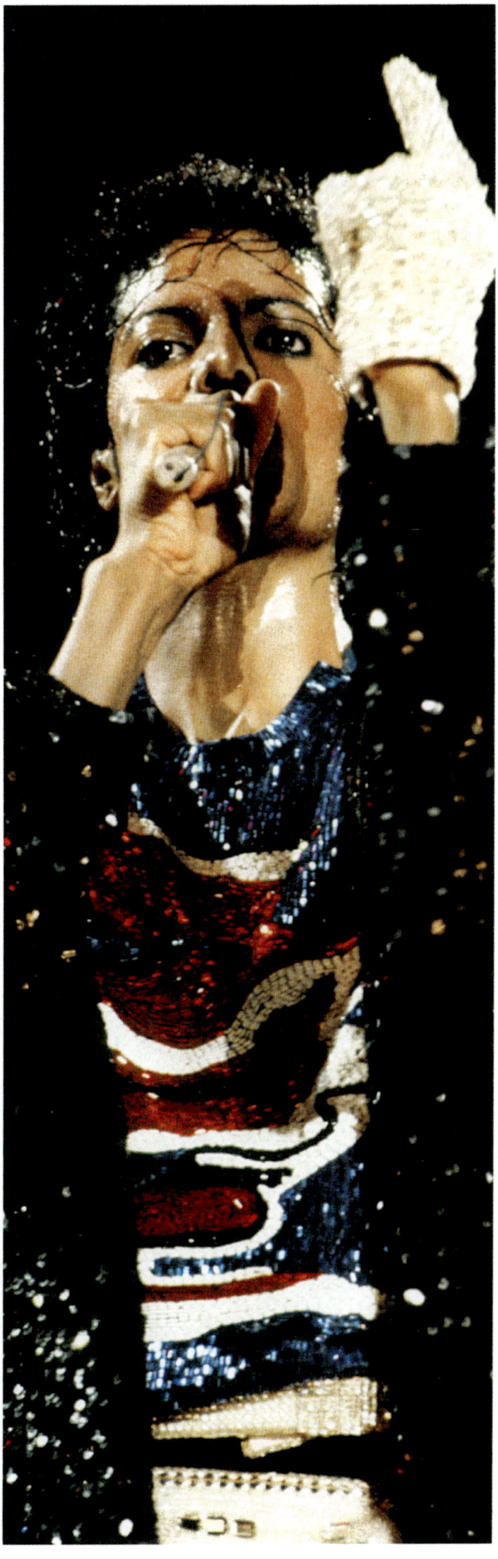

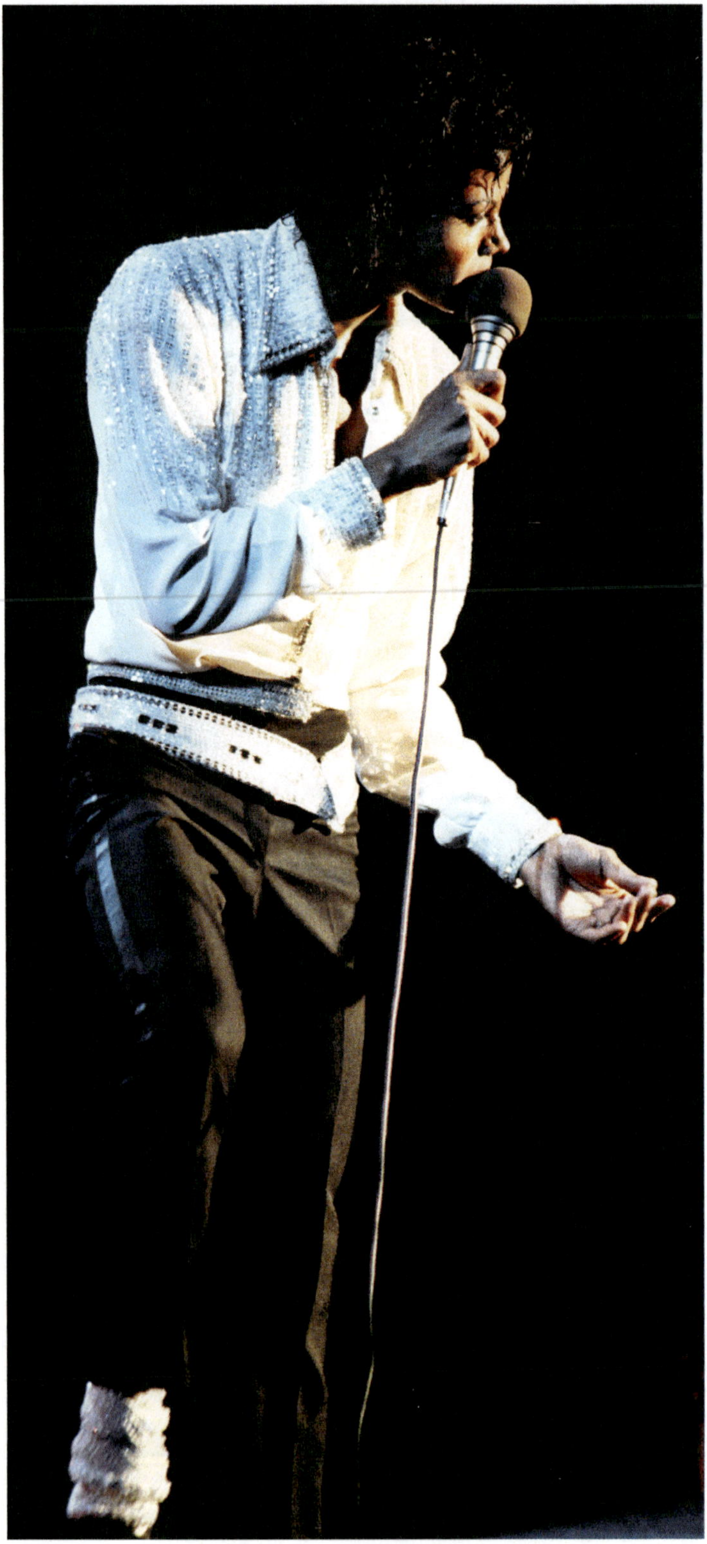

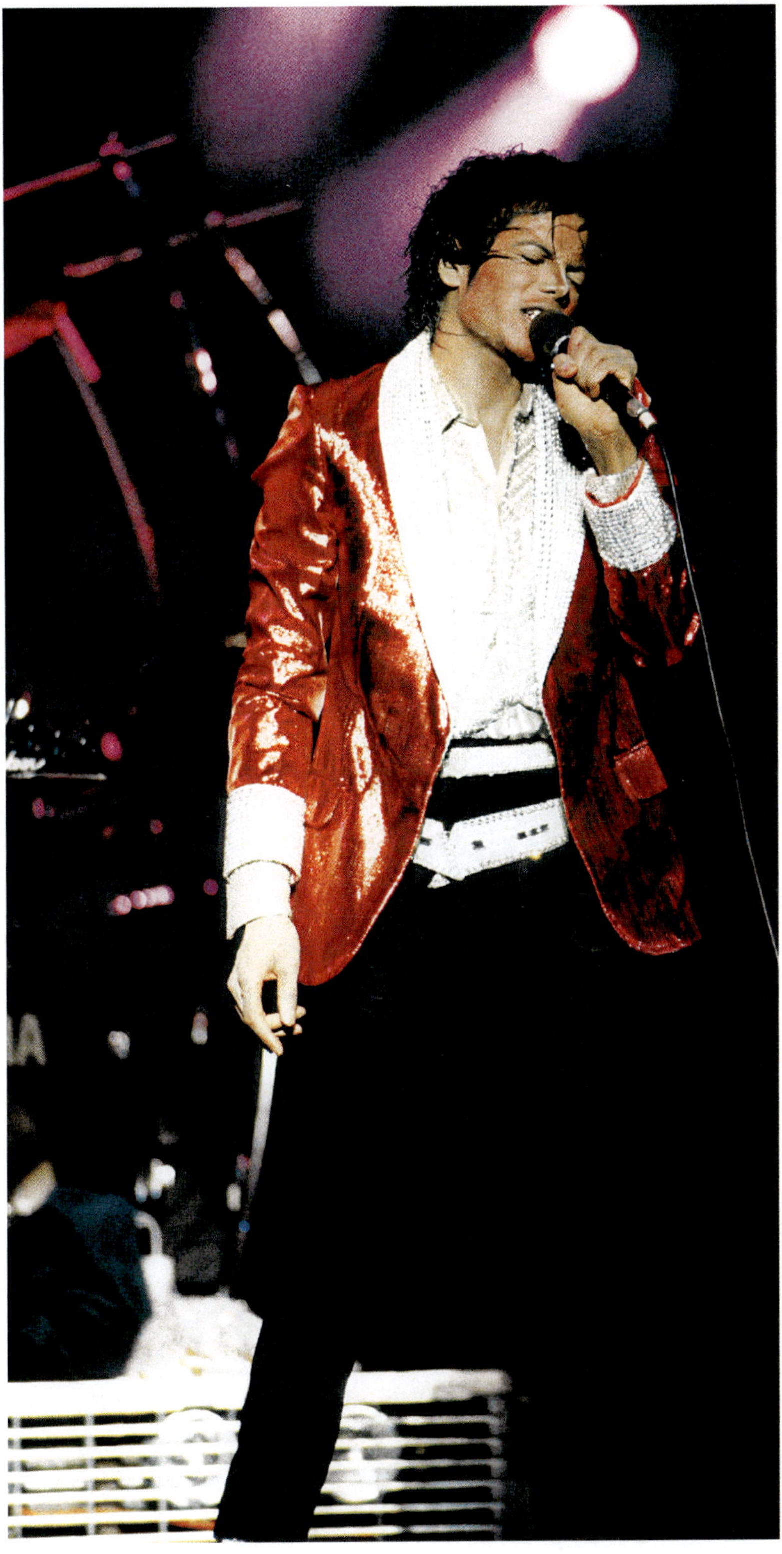

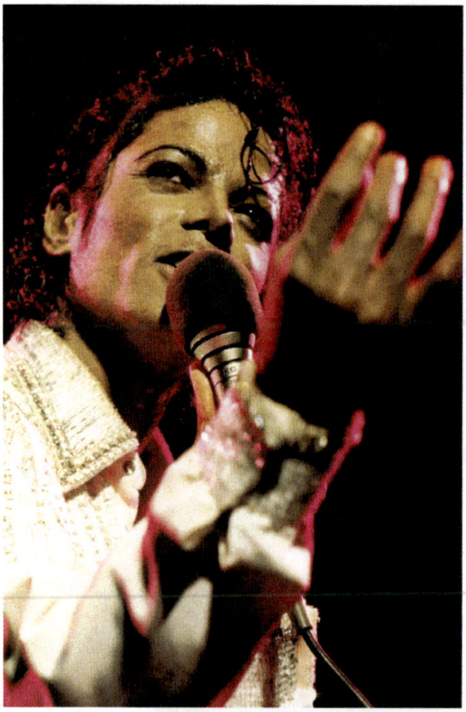

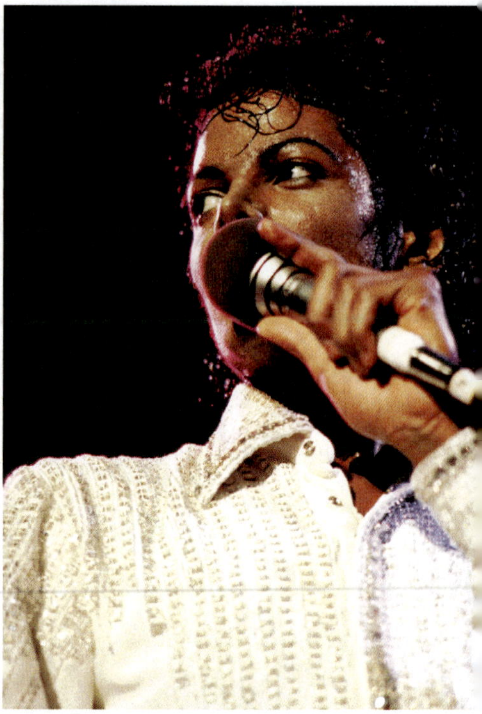

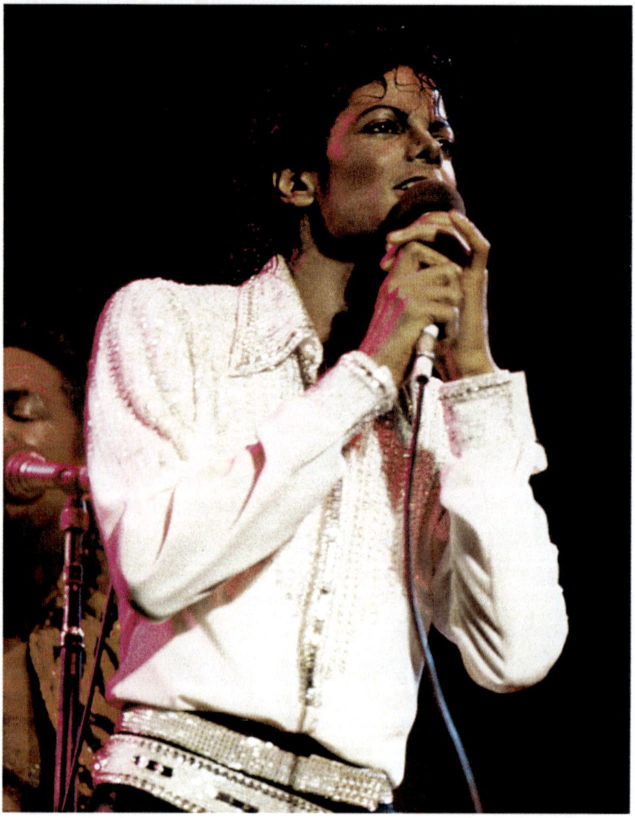

81

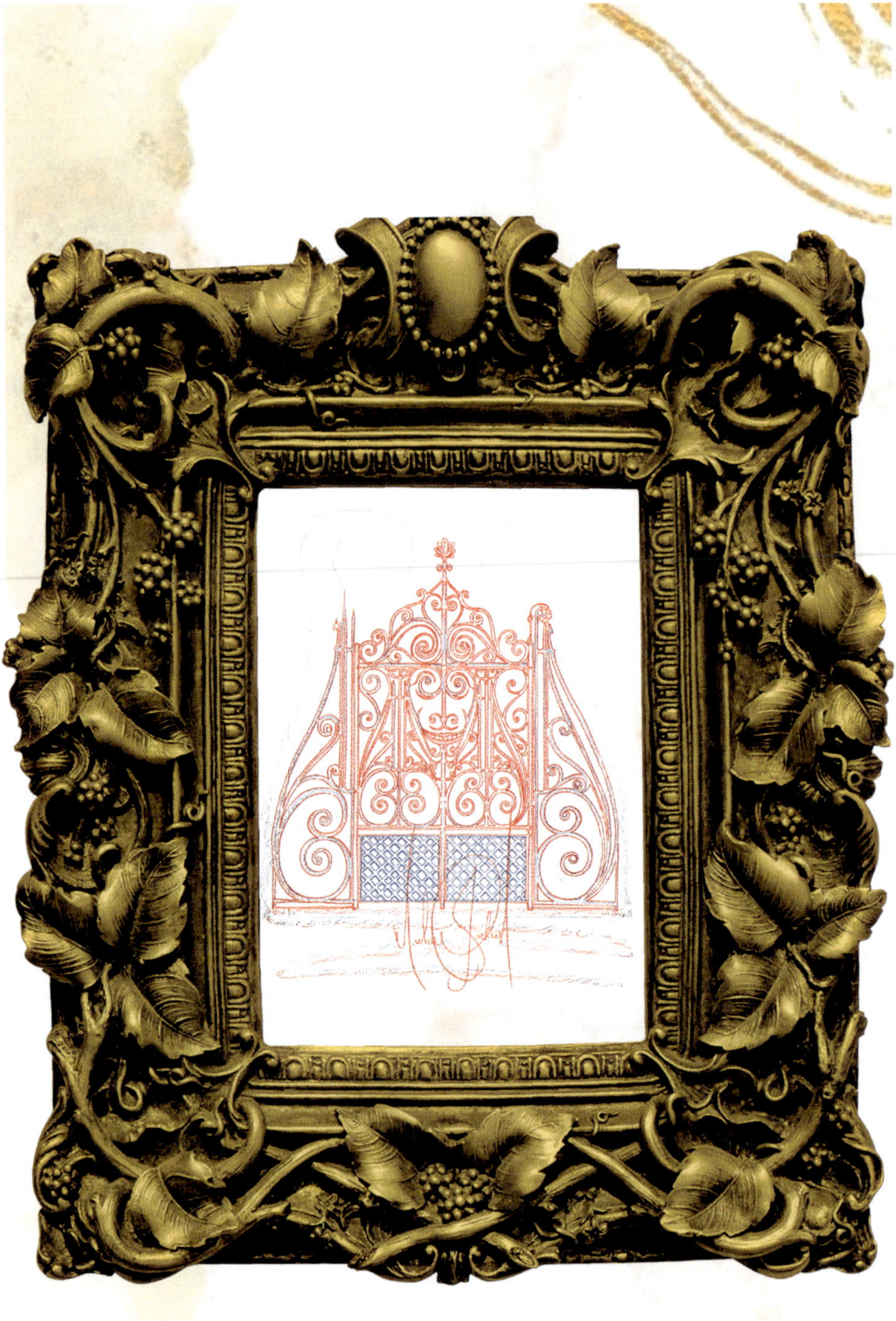

Alongside his many accomplishments, one of Michael's most valuable lessons—and lucrative ventures—was music publishing. Thanks to the guidance of Mr. Berry Gordy during the Motown years, Michael learned the immense value of owning his music and publishing rights, and he benefited from that knowledge.

Many people know the story of how my son purchased the Beatles catalog, a decision that strained his friendship with Sir Paul McCartney. Their relationship dated back to the early 1980s when Michael first met Paul during the *Wings* tour. The two eventually collaborated on songs like "*The Girl Is Mine*" and "*Say, Say, Say.*"

One of Michael's fondest memories with Paul was filming the music video for "*Say, Say, Say*" in 1983, featuring Paul, his late wife Linda McCartney, and my daughter LaToya. The video was shot on a 2,700-acre ranch that Michael fell in love with. He purchased the land and it became Neverland Ranch. Michael remained close to Paul and Linda for many years, after they first recorded music.

Michael faced a lot of criticism when he bought the Beatles catalog, which, I don't think was fair. I remember he came to me and said, "Our family will never have to worry about money again." He was right about this investment and many others that followed. Michael always had a good eye for business. He learned quickly from his mentors like Mr Gordy and Mr Jones.

Beyond the music industry, Michael had several other friends in the entertainment business who were close to him. Many of his friends visited him backstage during The Victory Tour, including actor Dick Gregory, Miko Brando, Mr. T., Yoko Ono, Julian Lennon, Diana Ross, Gregory Peck, and champion "Sugar Ray" Leonard.

Mr. Sammy Davis Jr. was dear friend and mentor to my son. They first met in Lake Tahoe, when Michael was admiring Sammy's watch, and Sammy generously gave it to him. This act of kindness left a lasting impression on Michael. After wearing the watch for several years, Michael gifted it to me, and I still wear it proudly.

Michael's generosity reflected the kindness of his mentors. It was common for him to give random gifts to family and friends, whether jewelry or items he wore that others admired. To me, his generousity was one of Michael's best qualities.

> **"**
> **Michael faced harsh criticism after buying the Beatles music catalog, which, I don't think was fair**

Left to Right: Michael, LaToya and Sir Paul McCartney

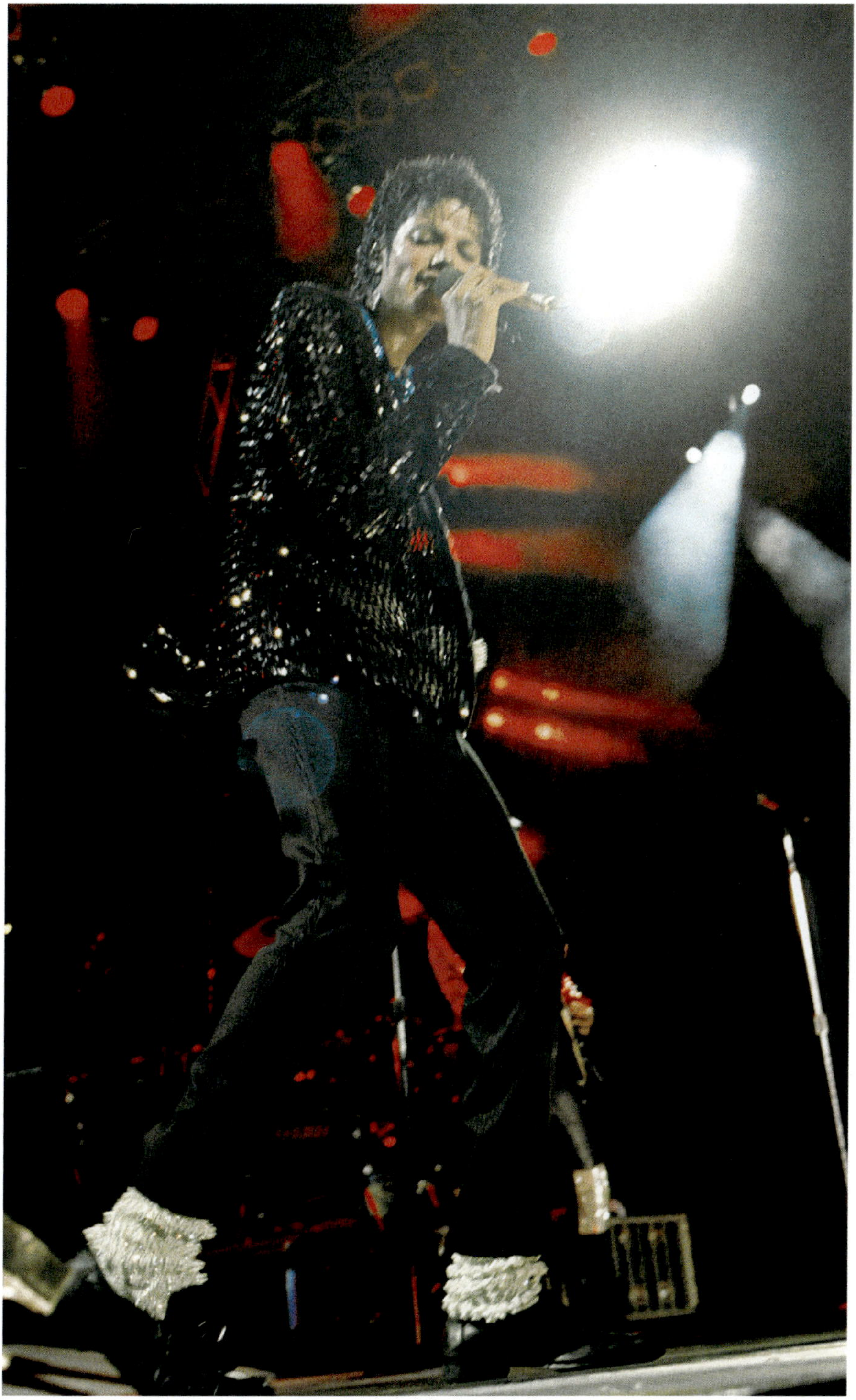

Left to Right: Joseph, Michael, Don King and Rev. Jesse Jackson

Michael and Dick Gregory

Michael; Sammy Davis Jr.

"Sugar" Ray Leonard and Michael;

90

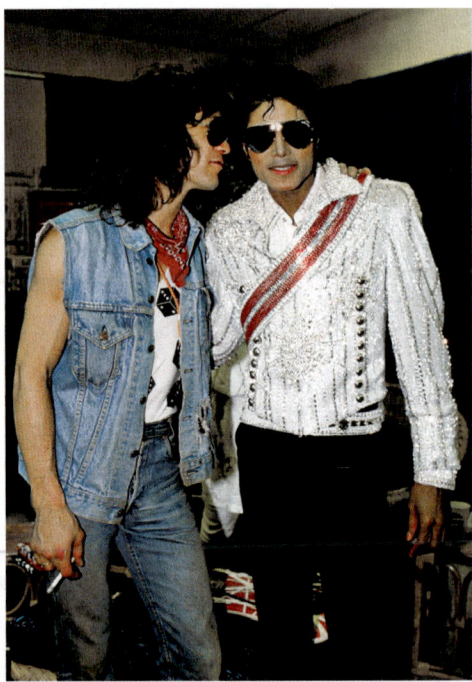

Backstage the Victory Tour: Eddie Van Halen, Michael and Randy

Backstage the Victory Tour: The Three T's, Michael and friends.

92

Emmanuel Lewis, LaToya and Michael

Left: Michael, Yoko Ono, Marlon and Julian Lennon   Right: Diana Ross, and Michael

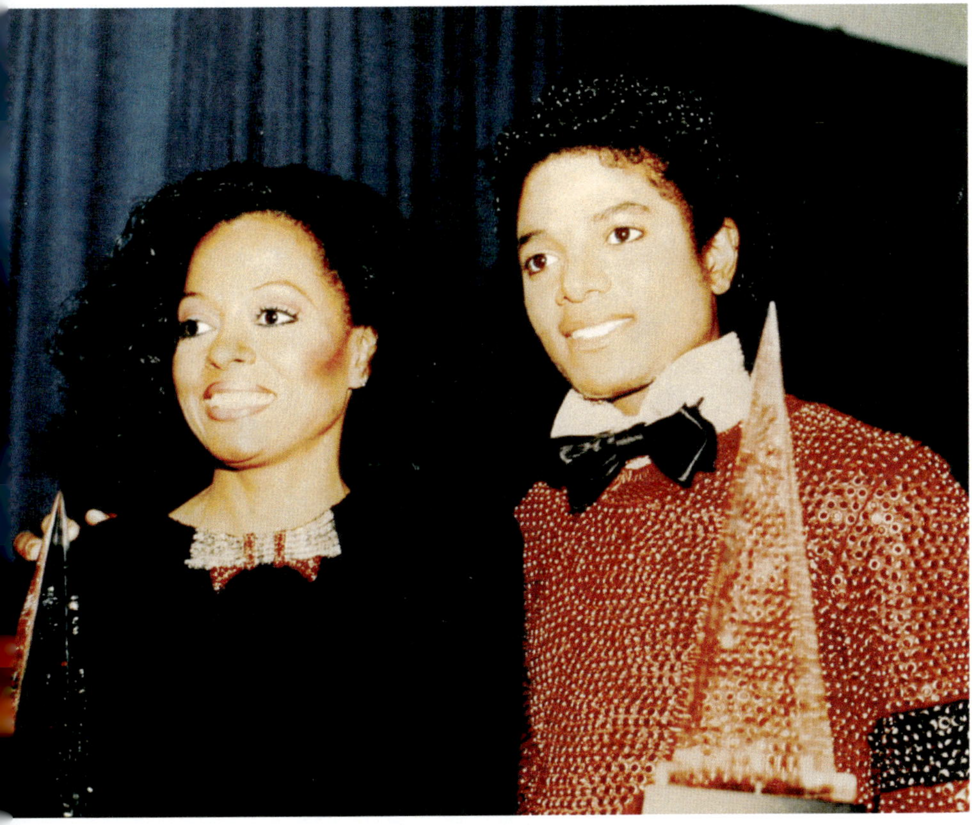

Left: Mr T. and the Three T's

Studio 54: Lionel Richie, Steve Rubell, (friend) Michael, and Debbie Allen.

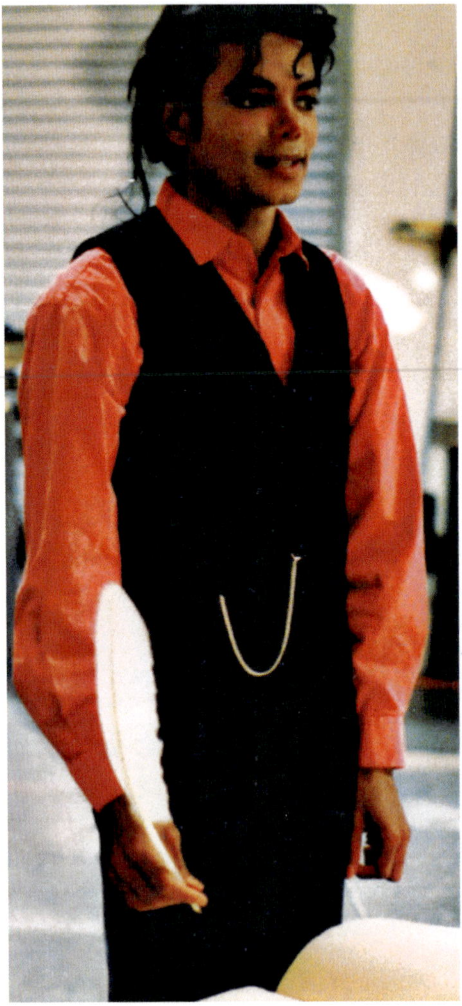

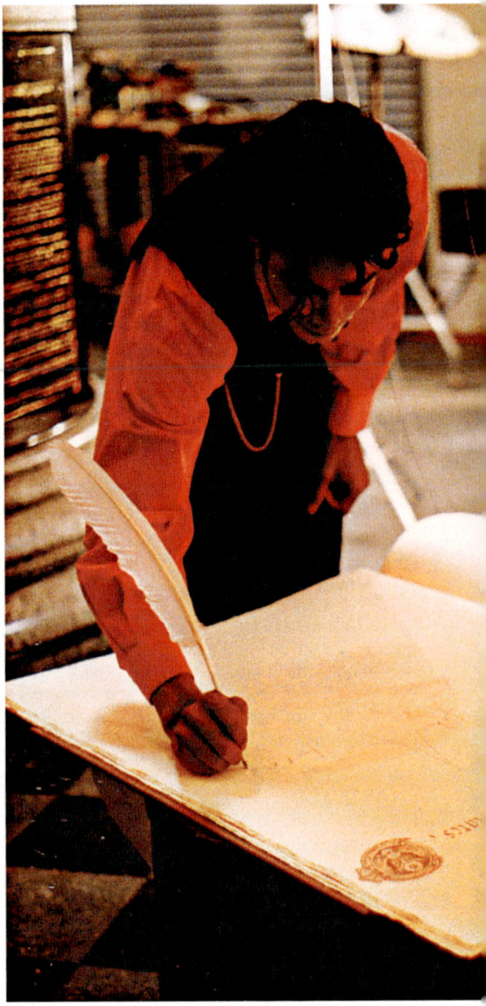

Left To Right: Marlon, Randy, Tito, Michael, Don King, Jermaine, Jackie and City Officials

Michael receives his star on the Hollywood Walk Of Fame as a Solo Artist in 1984.

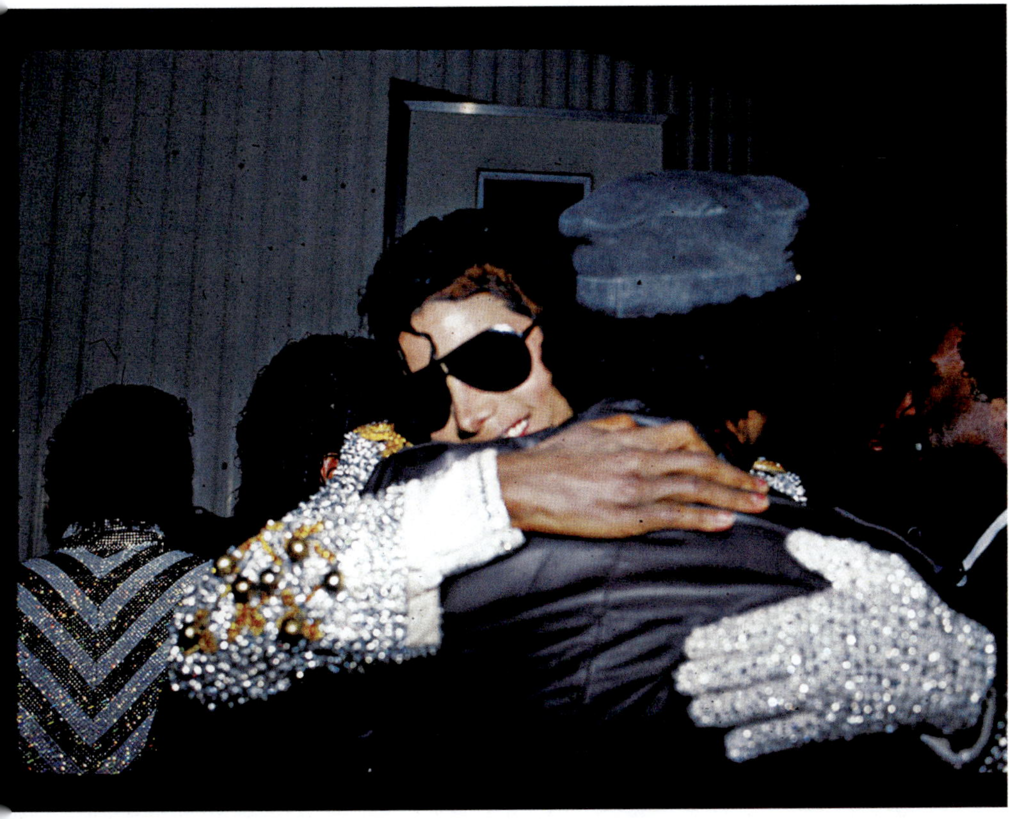

Boy

Michael Jackson 1994

I always told Michael, "You only get out of life what you put into it." I believe those words stayed with him. Michael had a clear picture of what he wanted to achieve and how far he wanted to go. He believed in hard work, humility, and kindness. No matter what he pursued in his career, he wouldn't settle for just being "good"—it had to be the best.

He used to tell me that an album shouldn't just have one good song; he believed that every song on the album should be a hit. And that's exactly what he achieved. He would spend countless hours in the studio, working until he was completely satisfied.

To stay motivated and to accomplish his specific goals, Michael often wrote notes to himself, reminders of his dreams. Sometimes, he would set a date for when he wanted his album to be a success. He wrote these notes on his mirror, where he could see them every day, using them as inspiration.

Michael always had big dreams for himself. He wanted to be the greatest entertainer the world had seen. I remember, before *Thriller* became a success, Michael said he wanted to create the biggest album of all time. I asked him, "How are you going to do that?" and all he said was, "Mother, wait, you'll see." Anyone who knew Michael knew he was like that—he wanted everything to be perfect. I used to tell him, "Man can't be perfect," but he wouldn't accept anything less. I don't know where he got it from.

As he grew older, he wanted to focus less on the business side of things. Learning from his mentors, Michael hired people to help manage his affairs, but he remained involved and always kept a watchful eye. Michael was trusting by nature, but, even when it was necessary to address any issues, confrontation wasn't in my son's character—he was too forgiving.

I didn't like when Michael was climbing in his career, and the media wanted to bring him down. They were on him like a blood hound. They called him terrible names in the press. My son was not a "Jacko." He could never get as far as he did in life and in his career if he were crazy, or stupid.

People often told me that Michael was more like me than his father. I used to tell Michael, "You can't be like me; you need to be stronger because you are a man." But he just couldn't bring himself to be that way. He allowed people to take advantage of him.

> **"I always told Michael, "You only get out of life what you put into it." I believe those words stayed with him.**

Michael receives his star on the Hollywood Walk Of Fame as a Solo Artist in 1984.

Michael receives his key to the city, with his manager at the time, Frank DiLeo

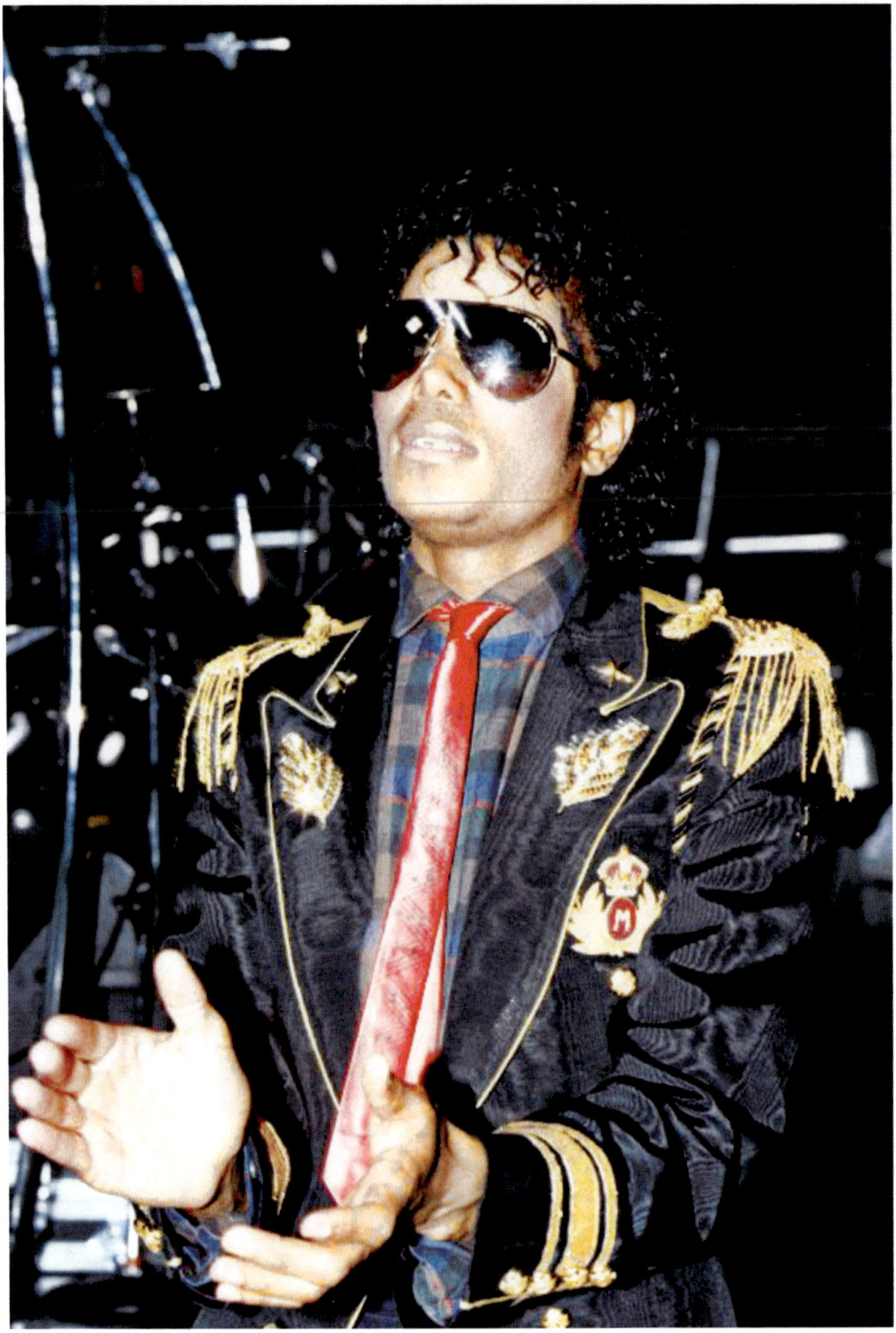

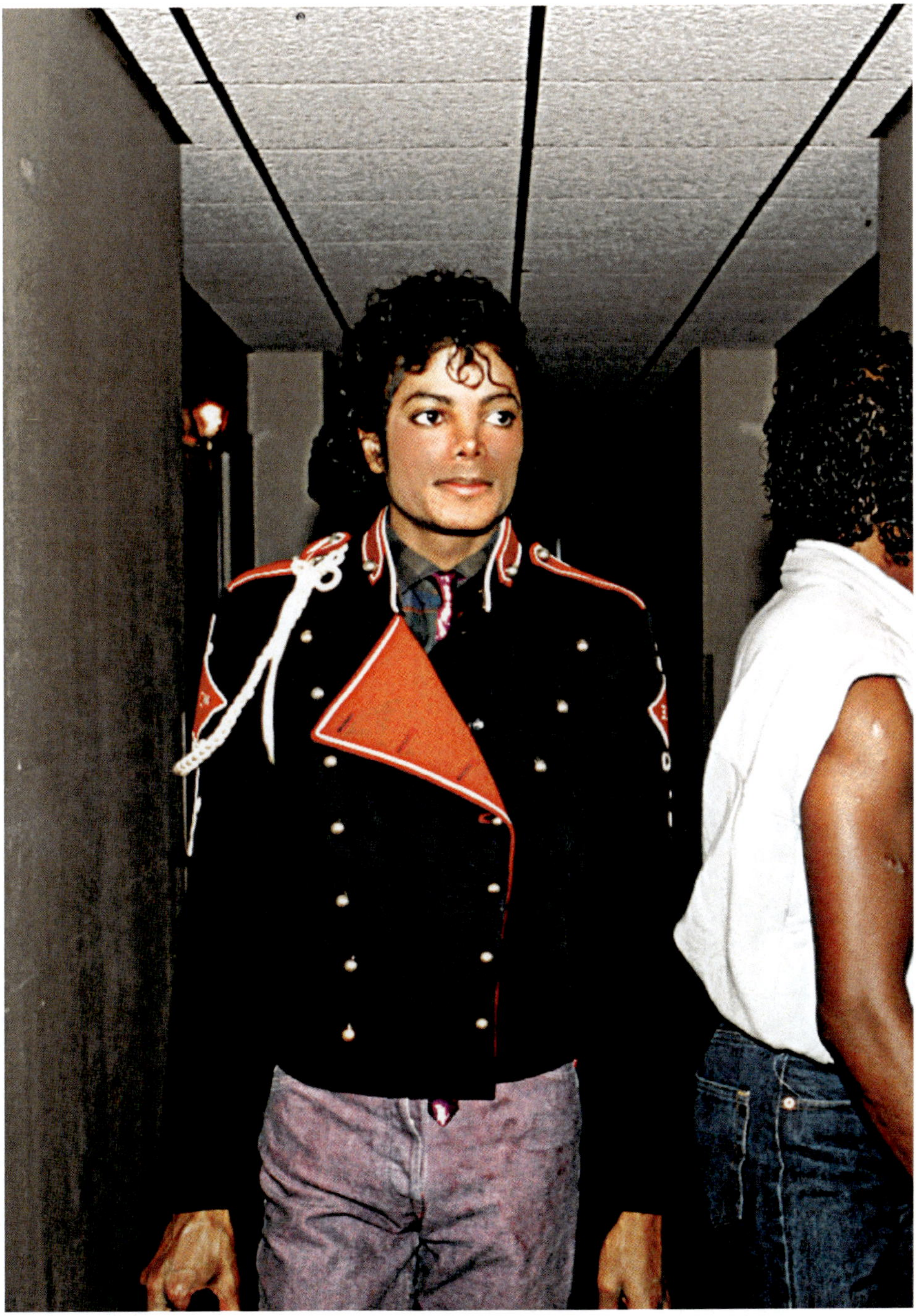

We the People of the United States,

Our backyard at home was basically a zoo for Michael's pets. He had a giraffe named Jabbar, named after basketball player Kareem Abdul-Jabbar, and a llama named Lola, after actress Lola Falana. He also had two deer, Prince and Princess, and a snake named Muscles. Michael kept all the animals outside in a sanctuary he built on the Encino property, except for one.

For years, Michael wanted a pet monkey. Naturally, I refused, until one day he brought home a baby chimp named Bubbles. Bubbles was different from the other animals we fostered. With his childlike demeanor, he would wave with his arms for us to pick him up. His intelligence was obvious the way he played games and teased the dogs in the yard. Bubbles lived and slept in a baby's crib in Michael's room; he was treated like one of the family, we all adored him.

Michael eventually moved to Neverland, but as Bubbles grew older, it became a challenge keeping him indoors at the residence. Bubbles was very well-trained, but he was becoming dangerously strong, and Michael's trainer told us that he could easily inflict harm without intending to. Sadly, Michael had to move Bubbles to a sanctuary where he could be cared for in a suitable enclosure.

Despite all the animals we had living on the property, you would never know they were there because Michael kept the animal sanctuary in immaculate condition.

When he moved to Neverland, Michael acquired even more exotic animals, like giraffes and tigers. His good friend, Dame Elizabeth Taylor, once gifted him with an elephant. With so many animals, Michael employed a staff of over 200 workers to care for his property and animals.

Neverland Ranch was surrounded by beautiful mountains. I was moved when I found out that Michael named those mountains after my husband and me. Classical music was always played around the ranch—it was one of the most peaceful places for Michael and all of us. He couldn't enjoy the outside world like everyone else, so he built a world behind those gates.

Michael opened his doors to many children, even when he wasn't at Neverland. What I want people to remember most about my son is his love for children.

Michael did everything he could to make a difference in people's lives, and I truly believe he succeeded, in so many ways.

> **What I want people to remember most about my son is how deeply he cared for others. He did everything he could to make a difference in people's lives, and I truly believe he did.**

Backstage at the Victory Tour with Michael and Magician Doug Henning

111

Top: Michael, my father and I; Bottom Michael, Jermaine, My father Prince, Marlon, Jackie and LaToya

If my son were still here today, I know he would be exploring new ventures—perhaps directing films, and acting.

Michael was responsible for many projects that people weren't even aware of. He collaborated with the city of Vegas to enhance the entertainment attractions, orchestrating light shows for hotel and contributing ideas such as building roller coasters and theme parks to attract more families during the slower seasons. Michael loved Vegas and it meant a lot to him when he received the key to the city. Michael lived in Vegas for some time with his kids before committing to his final concert, *This Is It*, at the O2 Arena in London, England.

Before Michael passed, he was privately studying film direction with a professor from California State University, and he encouraged his oldest son, Prince, to study with him. Paris was learning acting and singing, while Prince and Blanket (Bigi), were learning the art of film directing. Michael wanted all of three of his children, Prince, Paris and Blanket, to be skilled in the entertainment industry, teaching them not only the craft but also the importance of giving back to their community, through charity work.

After his passing, when Michael's children came to live with me, I was touched to see how naturally they embraced community service. They were eager to continue their father's work, delivering food and clothing to local shelters and those in need. Blanket, expressed a desire to support underprivileged communities in Africa and Asia. Michael had taken his children around the world—to places like Asia, Bahrain, and Japan—giving them a broader understanding of the world, which made me proud. He carried on the values that my husband, Joseph, instilled in him as a child.

Most people don't know the origin of Michael's sons' names. "Prince" was actually after my father, Prince Albert Scruse. Michael was very close to his grandfather, which is why both of his sons, Prince Michael Joseph Jackson and Prince Michael Jackson (Blanket/Bigi),were both named Prince.

While Michael often said that he didn't have a childhood, in my opinion, he did—he had his brothers, and together they had moments of fun and innocence, but, of course, show business placed obligations on him that other children didn't have.

Joseph was strict —as many parents were back then—and given where we came from in Gary, Indiana, it was necessary to ensure our children stayed away from crime that was prevalent in the streets. Joseph achieved that through music.

As Michael's mother, I can't dwell on regrets about his childhood; When Michael entrusted his children to me, I made sure they took their time before entering show business, allowing them to experience a childhood in a way that he never truly could.

> **"**
> **While Michael often said that he didn't have a childhood, in my opinion, he did—though not the carefree one he might have wished for.**

Top: Michael, Joseph, Randy, Janet, Marlon and Jackie   Bottom: Me and Michael visiting with family

Top: Joseph, Michael, Me, Rebbie, Randy, celebrating with family Bottom: Randy and Michael with cousins

Top: Michael with his family. Bottom: Janet, Michael, Marlon, Joseph and Jackie (at Janet's graduation);

Top: Michael, Joseph and Randy. Bottom: Michael, LaToya, her friend, and me

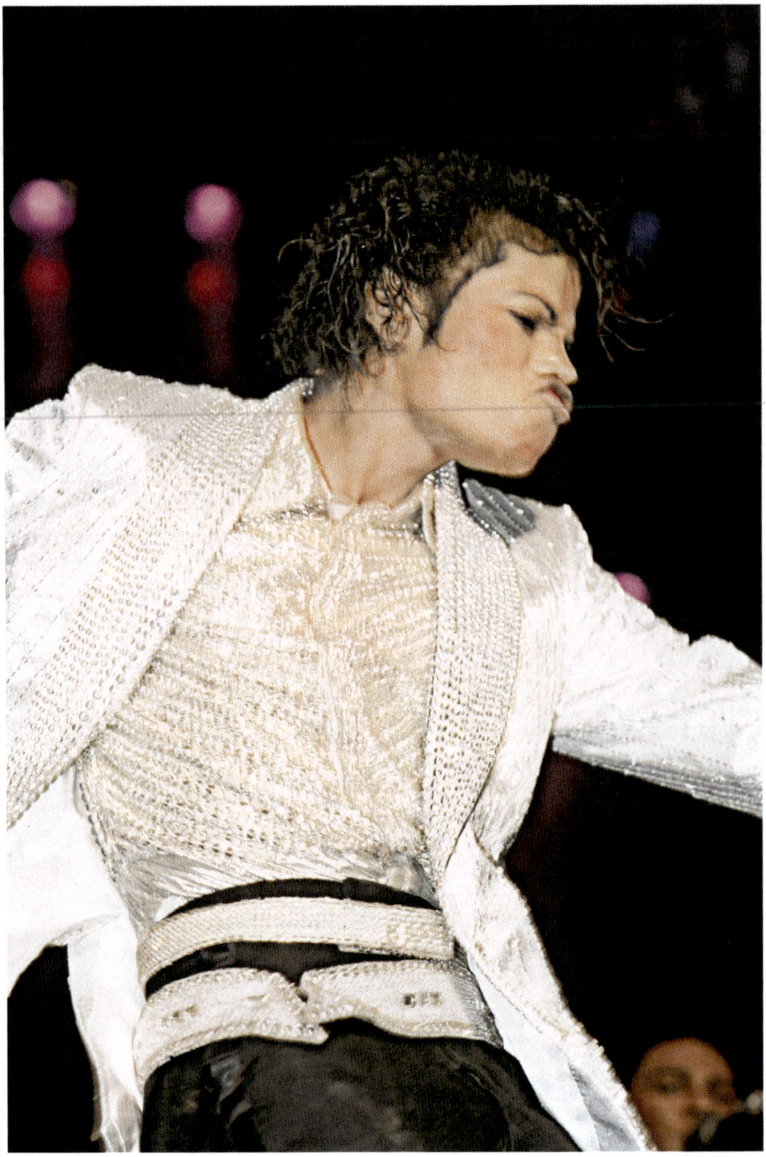

Michael, Bubbles, family and friends

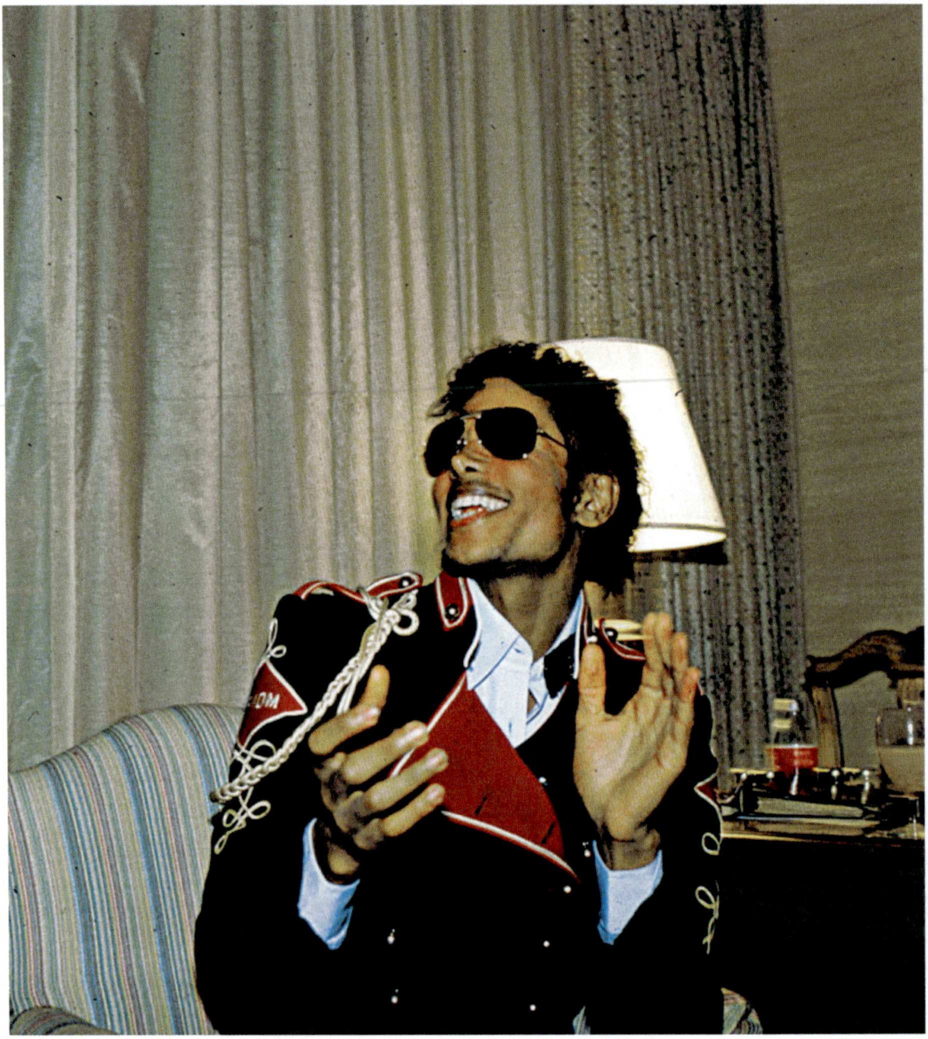

If there's one thing I know for sure, it's how much my son adored his fans. I will never forget the years when Michael faced trial in 2005. Each morning, we for the courthouse, and every day, fans would gather at the gate, showing their support with signs, gifts, and prayers.

It touched both Michael and me to see Bible verses on signs, filled with loving words of encouragement, urging him to stay strong during such a difficult time. The trial was one of our biggest struggles. Every day, I prayed for the truth, that my son would be free, because I knew he was innocent. His fans knew as well.

One thing Michael would always tell his his security guards and staff was to "always be gentle with my fans," no matter what.

When Michael still lived at home, there were always several fans waiting at the gate. Occasionally, one would sneak into the yard to see him, and sometimes even into the house—in fact, incidents like these inspired his lyrics to *Billy Jean*. Anytime fans intruded, Michael remained calm and polite. Even the large crowds didn't faze him. He was genuinely grateful to his fans, always acknowledging that he wouldn't be who he was without their love and support.

I have been close to my son throughout his life. Our bond grew stronger after his brothers left home, and it deepened as we battled his trials. I understood that Michael needed our family at the courthouse just as much as he needed his fans, so I remained by his side, every day.

In later years, when I faced a trial for the wrongful death of my son against the concert promoters, AEG, Michael's fans were with me every step of the way. Every morning when I arrived at the courthouse, and when I left, they were there to show their support for our family. I can never thank the fans enough for their unwavering love and encouragement.

There are things about Michael that his fans know which often surprise me. In fact, on the day he passed away, it was one of his fans who first called to tell me they had seen an ambulance leaving Michael's home in Bel-Air. Initially, I didn't want to believe it. I was in complete denial, and said, "Please don't scare me; it could be anyone. It doesn't have to be Michael." Soon after, I hung up the phone, my husband called to confirm the news, urging me to get to the hospital because Michael was being taken in an ambulance.

When I arrived to the hospital, I found everyone quiet in the room. Then I saw a man I hadn't seen before, I was told his name was Dr. Murray. He was waiting, but he said nothing to me, nor the family about what happened to Michael. Not a single word. Dr. Murray told the media that he consoled me, but that was a lie.

Finally, the doctor entered the room, and as silence enveloped us, I asked, "Well? Did he make it?" The doctor replied, "No, he didn't make it." All I remember after that was a scream escaping my lips, and then I must have blacked out because I cannot recall what happened afterward. It's a blur.

No parent should have to bury their child. Not a day goes by when I don't think about Michael.

> **If there's one thing I know for sure, it's how much my son loved his fans. He would always say, '*I love you more*'**

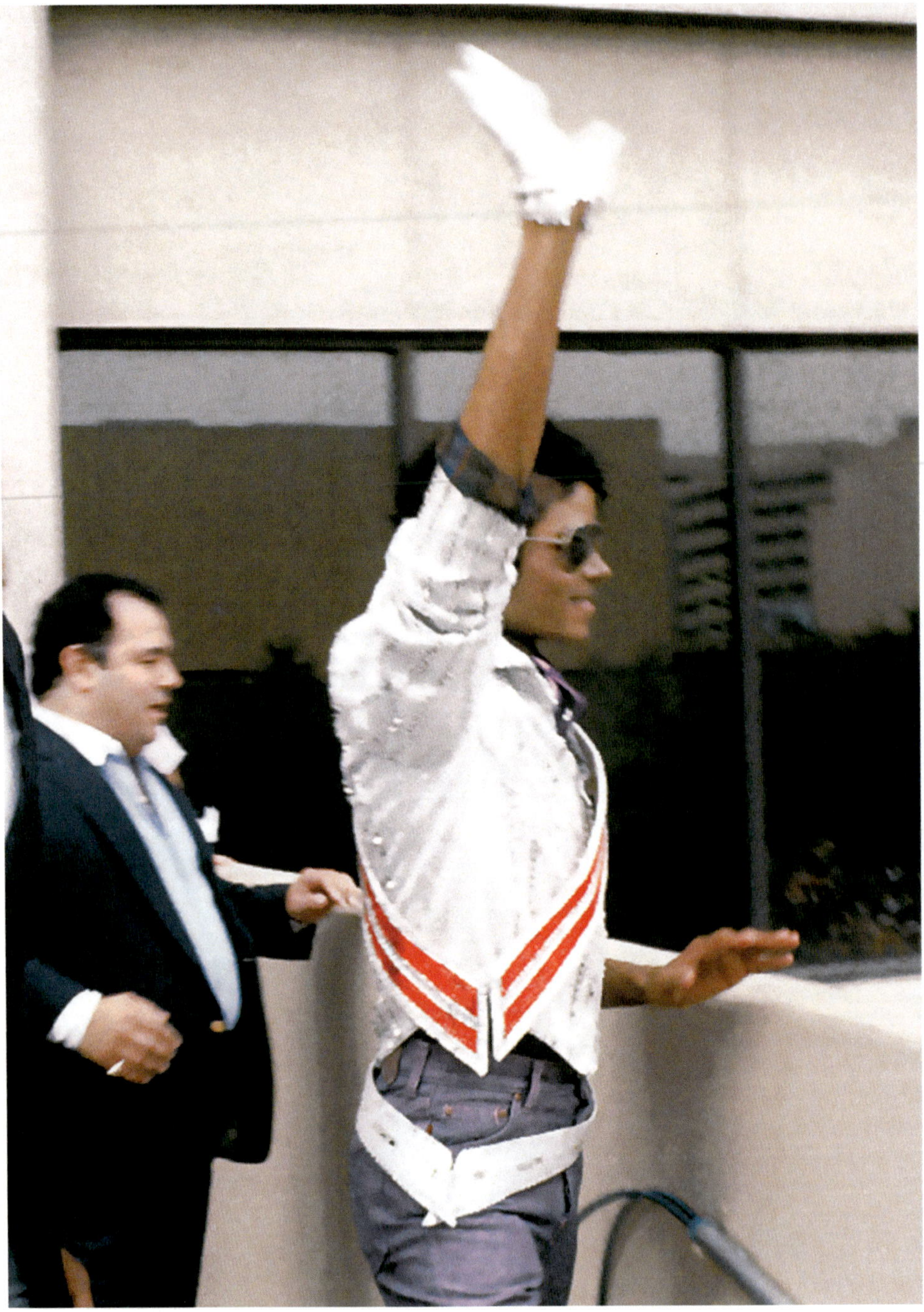

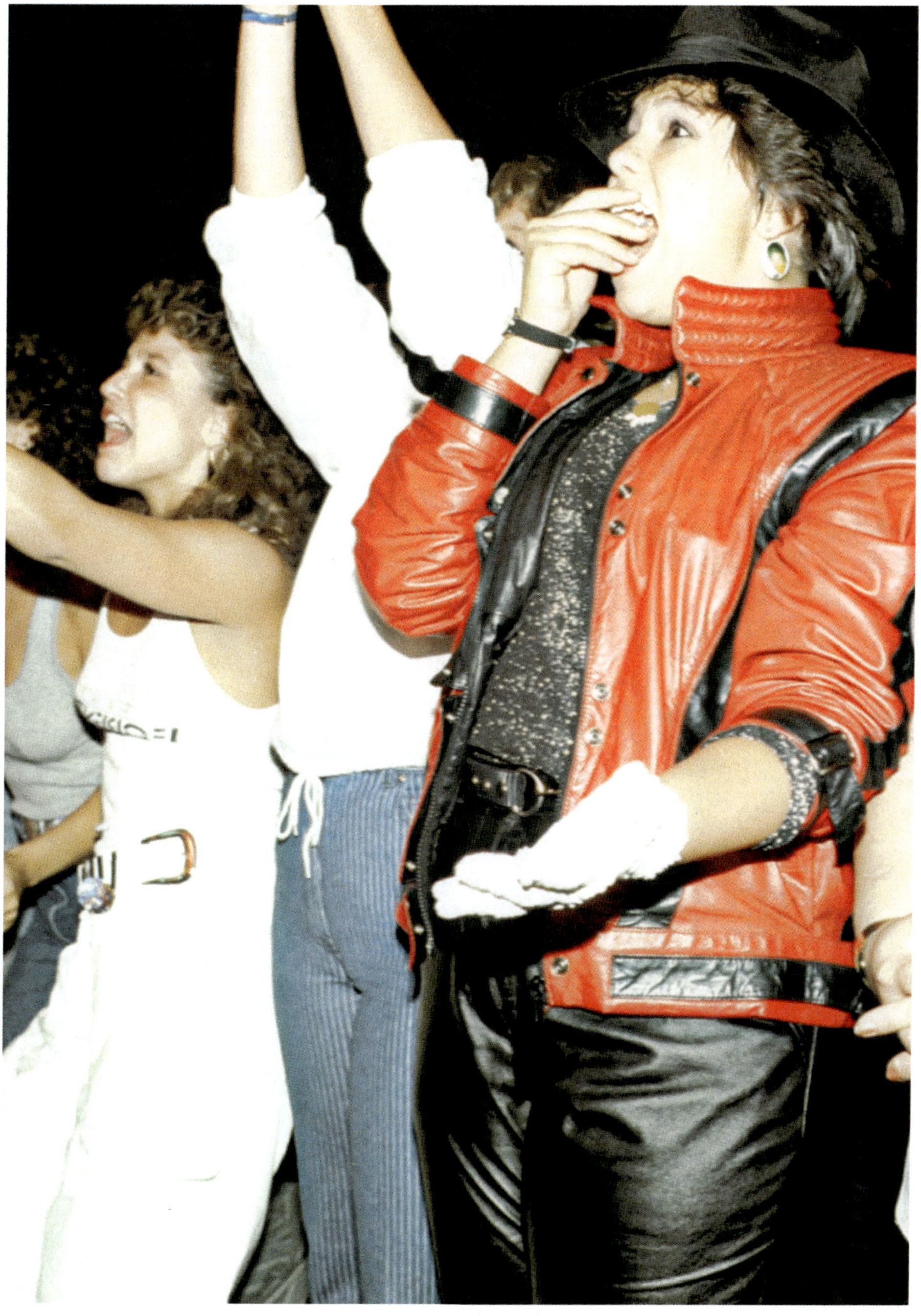

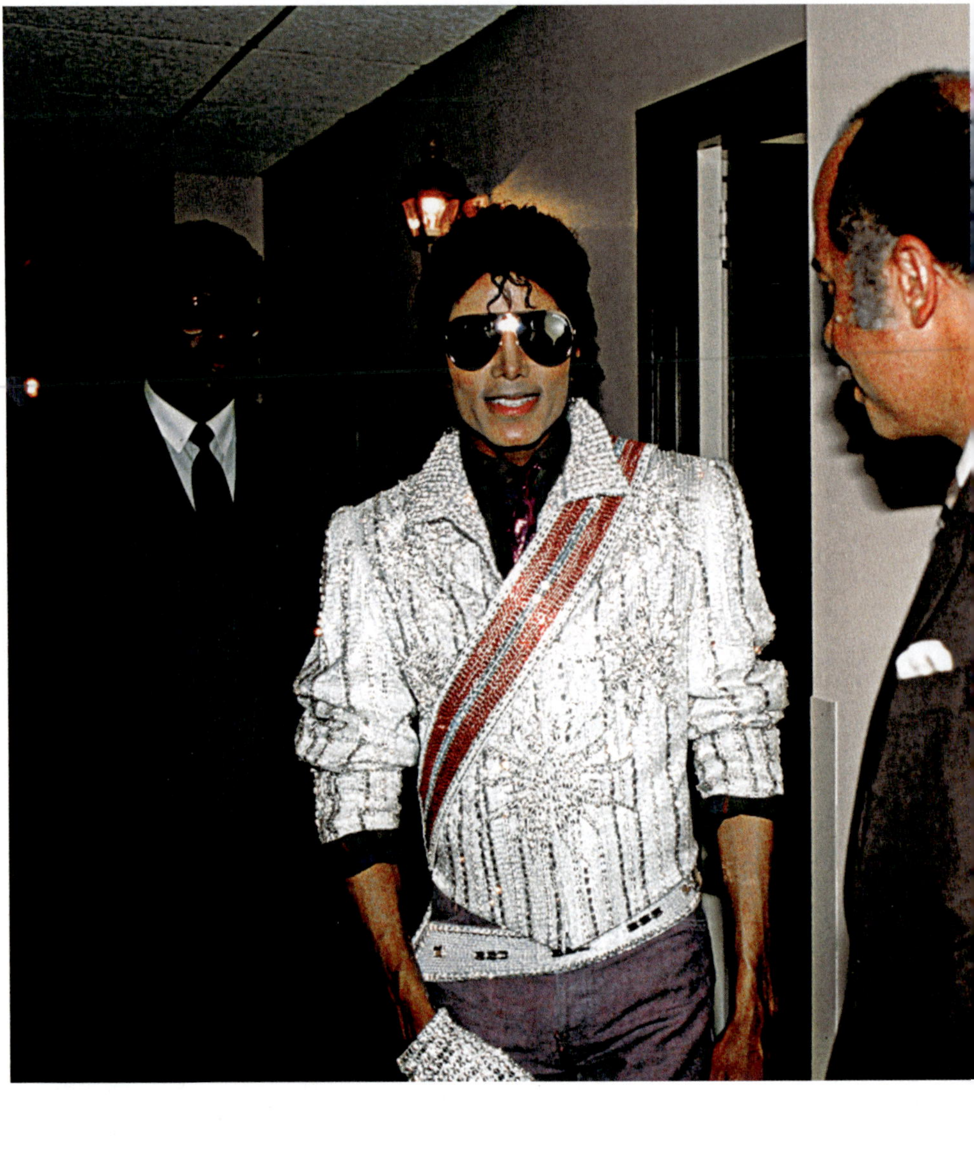

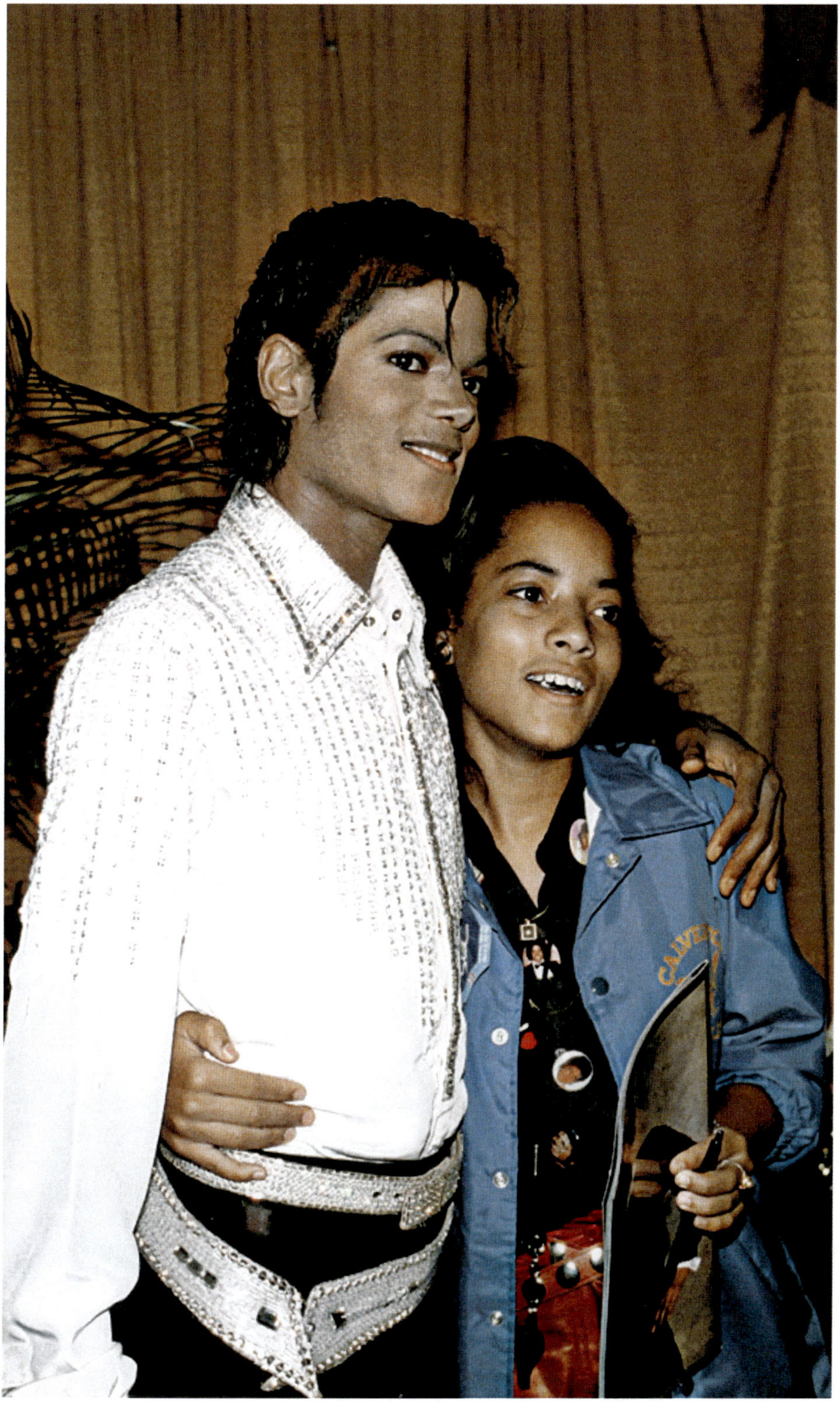

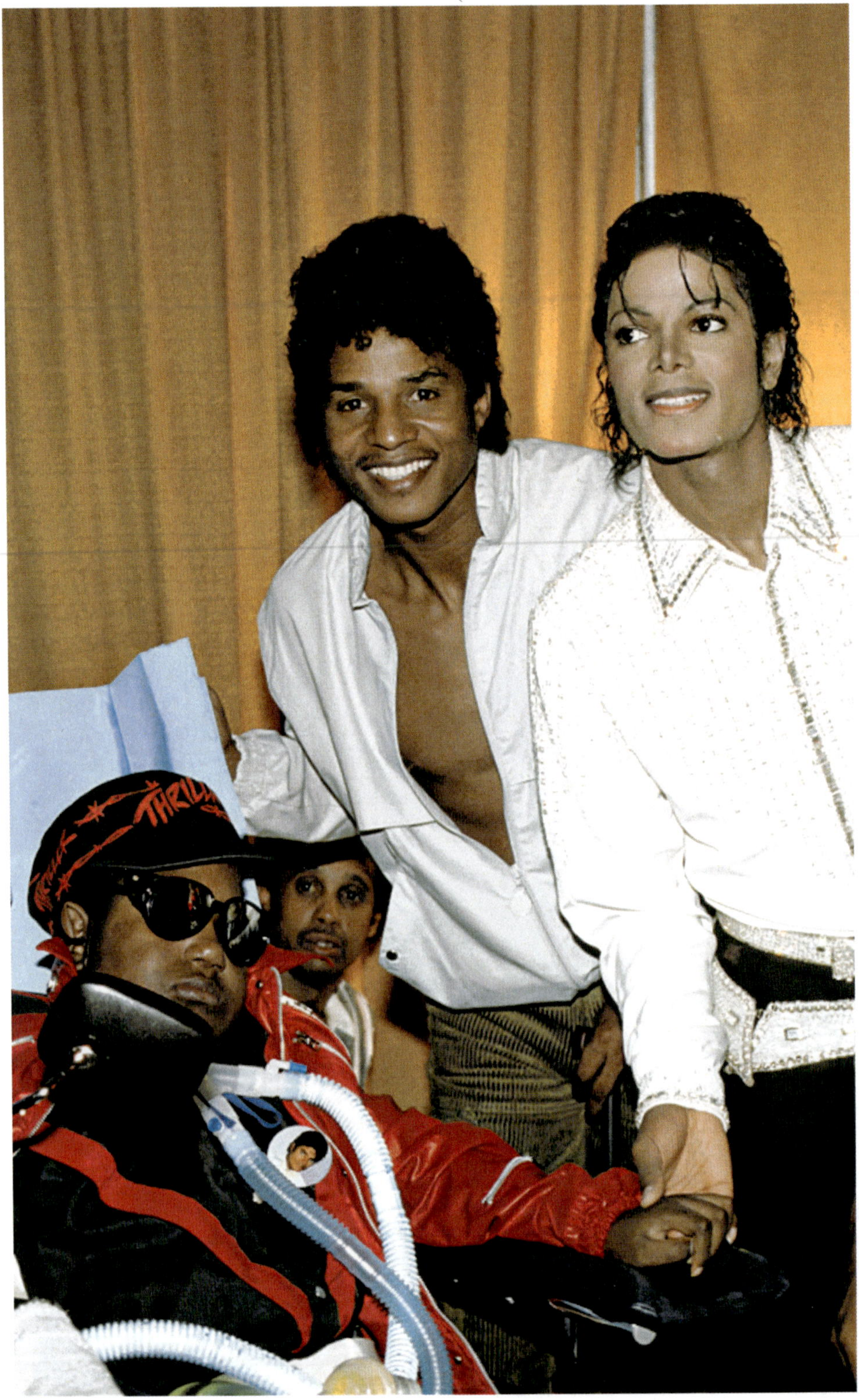

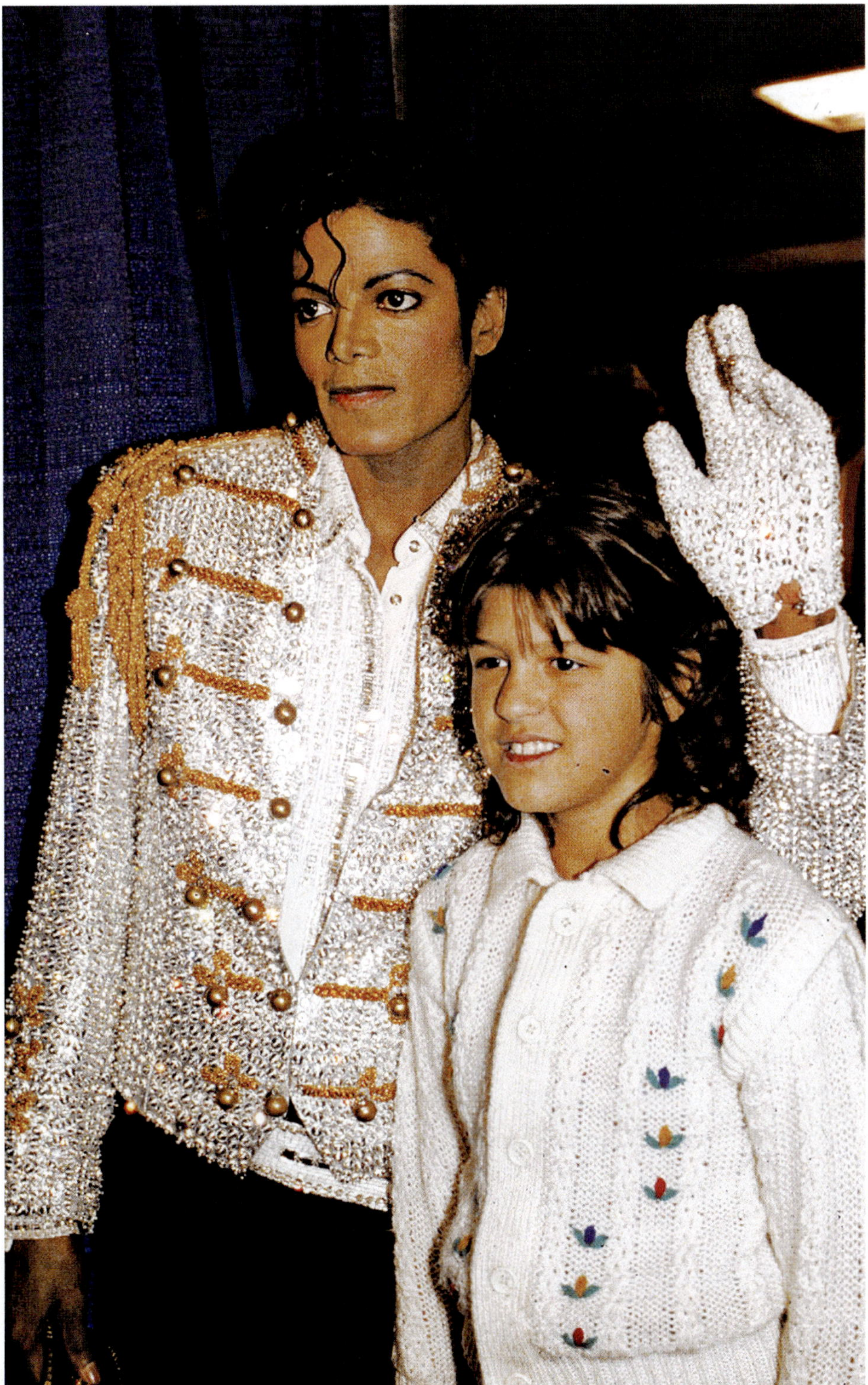

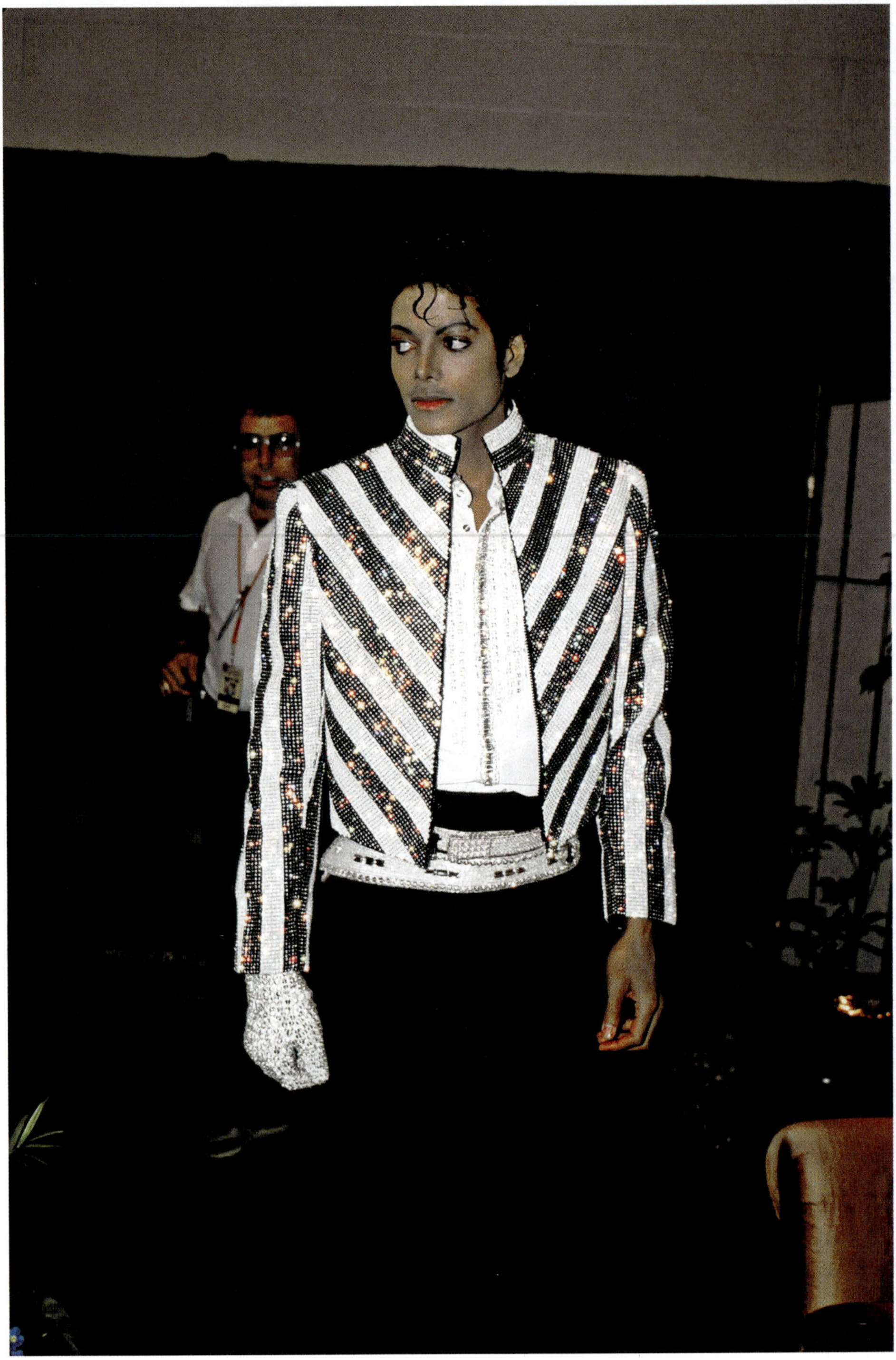

129

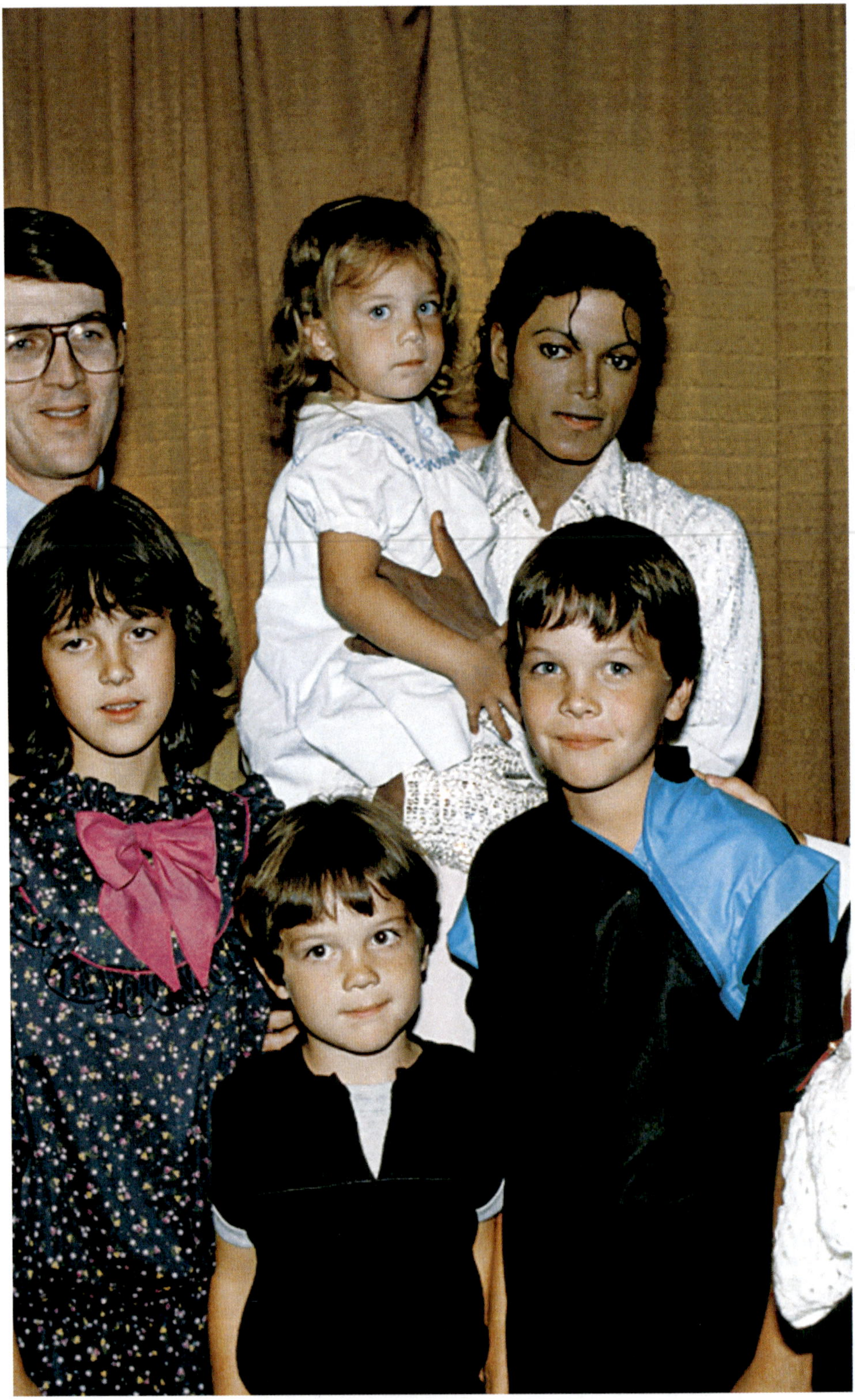

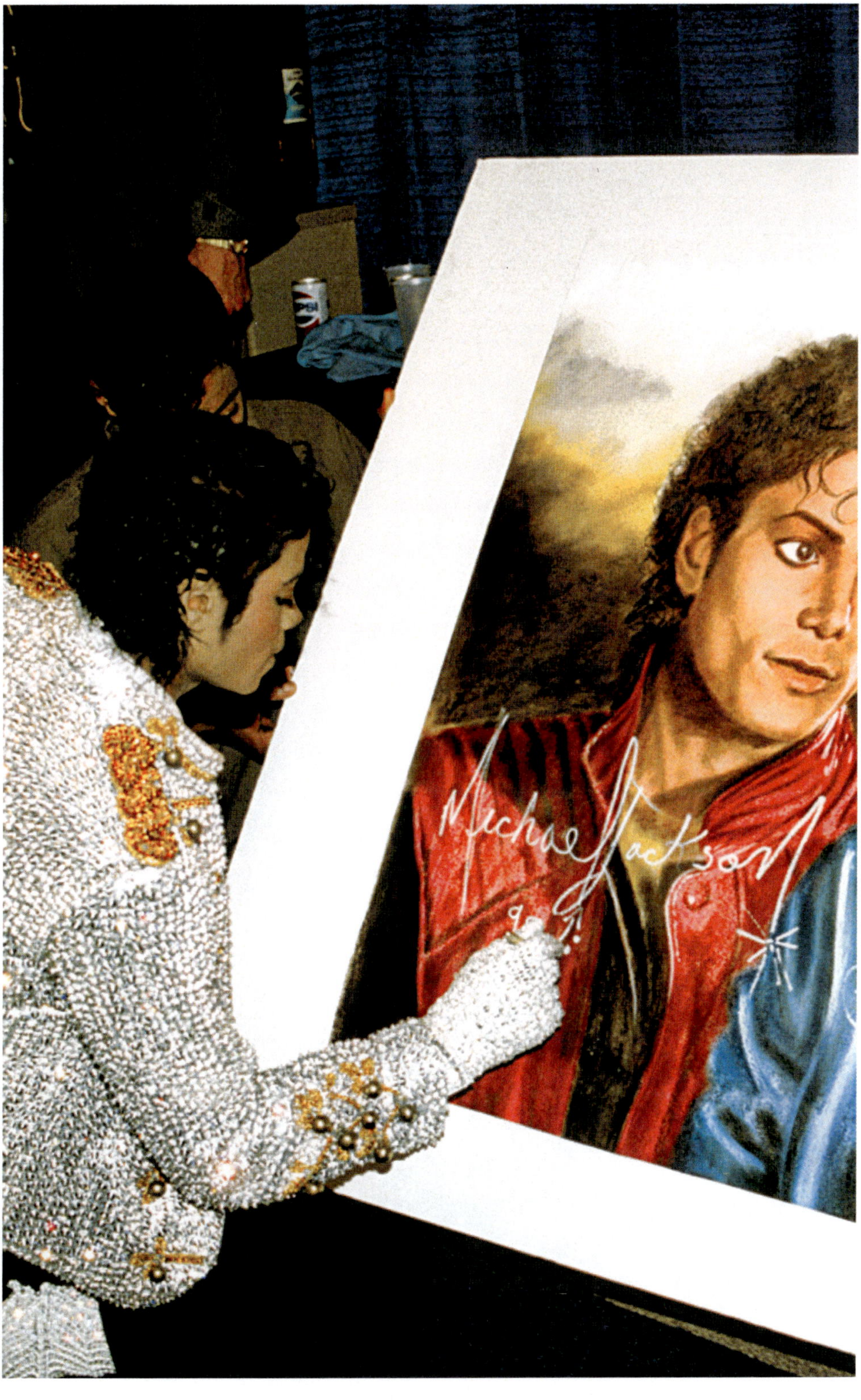
Michael Jackson

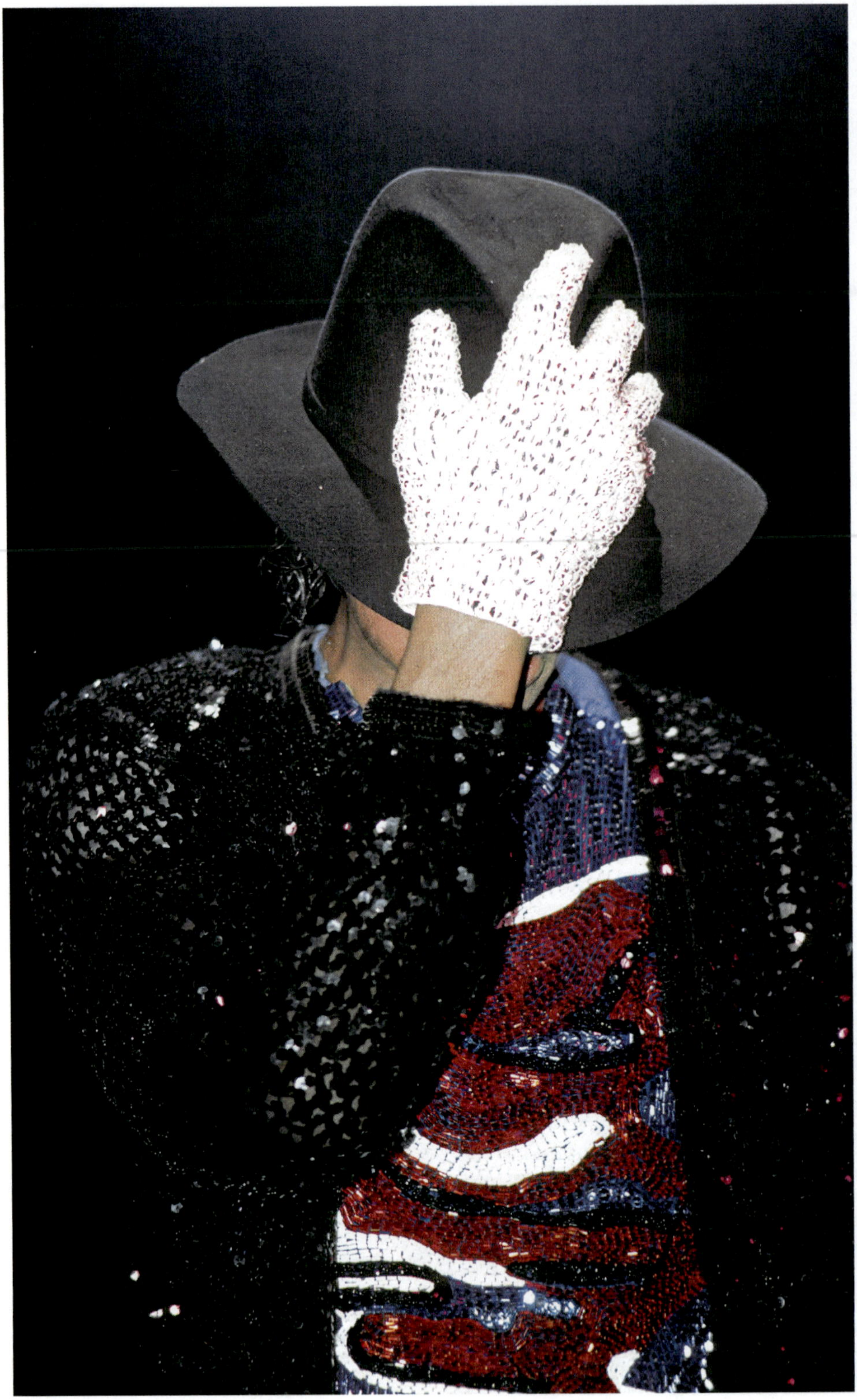

My son lived an extraordinary life and was profoundly grateful to be able to pursue his passion through music. However, both my husband and I know that Michael's fame did not come without a price.

I can't speculate on what could have been done differently if we could turn back time. My son would still be alive today if he had people around him whom he could trust. Dr. Murray was negligent. He was responsible for my son's care. You simply cannot treat your patient's life so carelessly. I have many questions along with suspicions regarding the doctor's behavior and claims, which he showed little remorse.

The man responsible for Michael's death is still alive and free. His mother is able to look him in the eye and tell him she loves him. I can't do that. No amount of time Dr. Murray spent in jail will ever bring my son Michael back.

Most people definitely misunderstood Michael. Few truly knew who he was. Regardless of what some may think, Michael was a kind person, a good son, and he was the best father to his children. We continue to share our stories with Michael's children and his fans because I know he would want them to understand how much they truly meant to him.

The media was unfair to my son, and many people around him lied on him, creating stories out of greed and a desire for money. That was all they wanted from Michael—money.

As Michael's mother, I knew who he was; my son was not a child molester. He loved children and often said he would rather "slit his own wrists than ever hurt a child." My son was not a freak; he was not the unstable person they tried to portray him as. They made fun of his appearance and said he wasn't proud of being who he was. It broke my heart.

As Michael's mother, I know that Michael underwent many surgeries, especially on his nose, which upset me greatly. I do understand that Michael had a problem with not knowing when enough was enough. Sometimes I would call his doctors and beg them not to operate on Michael's nose. I even went as far as asking them to put him under and bandage him up, without doing the surgery. But every time I saw my son again, I knew the doctors hadn't listened and were continuing to do further procedures on my Michael's nose.

> **"**
> **Most people misunderstood my son. Few truly knew who he was. Michael was a kind person, a good man, and he was a good father to his children.**

No matter his insecurities, Michael did everything he could to help people. This is what he cared about most. This is how I wish for my son to be remembered: as a good person. I remember the day Michael was born, when the doctor handed him to me, crying. I remember every moment from Michael's first day, to his last.

I am praying for that day when I will see my son Michael again. A mother should never outlive her child; the pain is deep. There's not a day that passes when I don't think about all who I have lost, but I get through it with prayer.

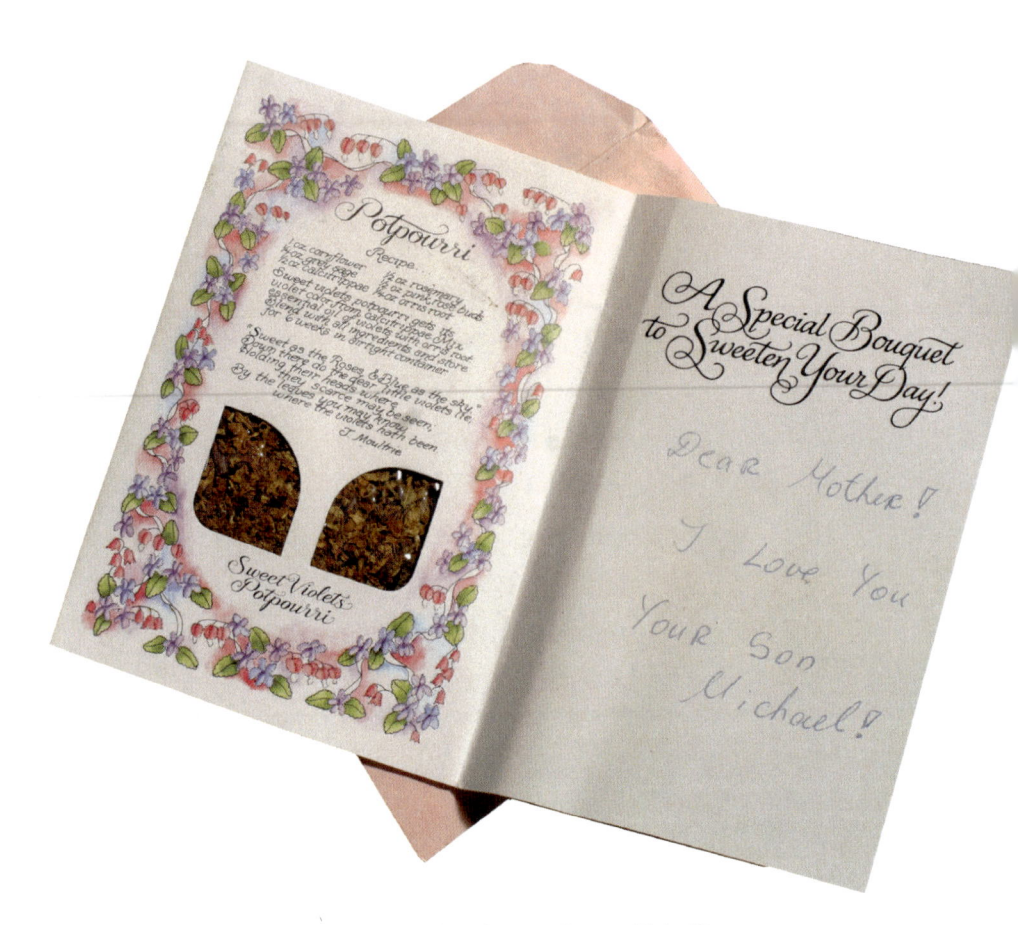

"Dear Mother! I love you. Your son Michael!"

135

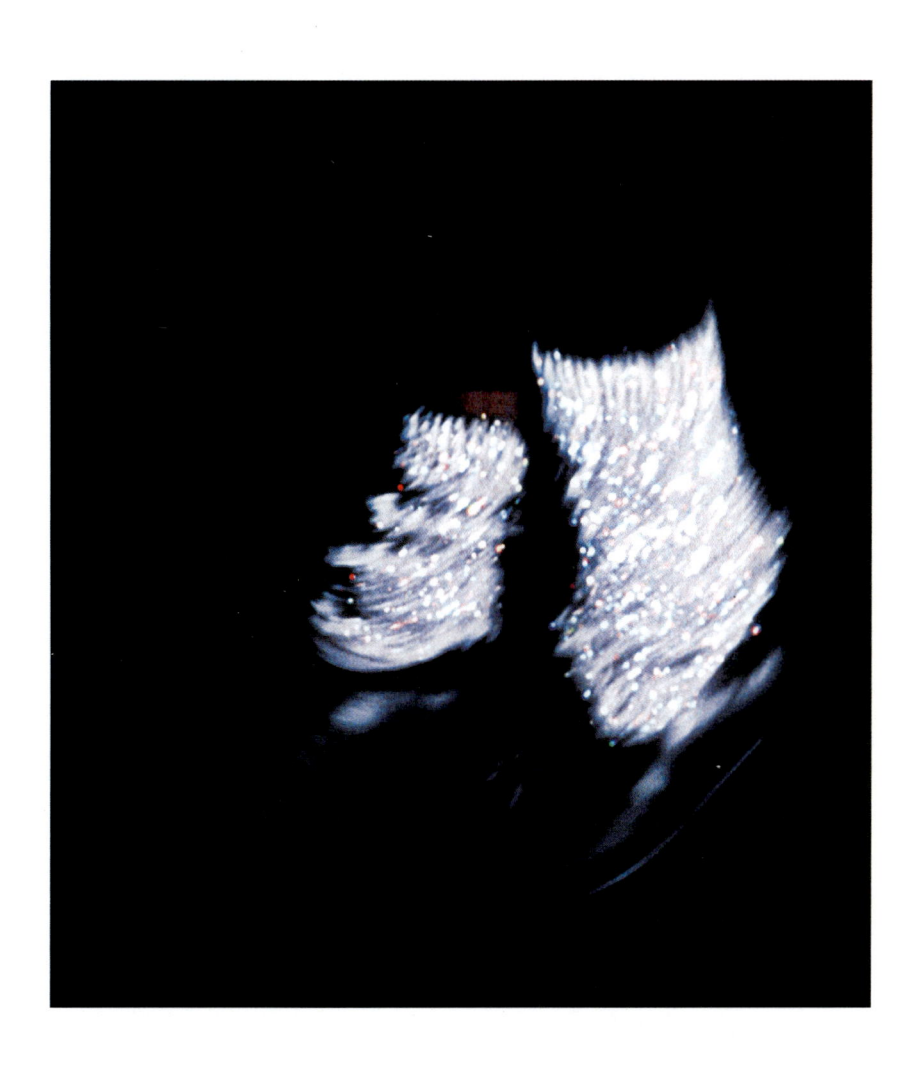

Made in the USA
Las Vegas, NV
01 April 2025